Emma's Gift

Furry Friends through Many Lifetimes

Katherine Mayfield

ISBN # 978-0-9976121-6-5

Cover photo by Adele.

Also by Katherine Mayfield

The Box of Daughter: Healing the Authentic Self

*The Meandering Muse: Uncommon Views
of Everyday Things*

Bullied: Why You Feel Bad Inside and What to Do About It

*Stand Your Ground: How to Cope with
a Dysfunctional Family and Recover from Trauma*

*Dysfunctional Families:
The Truth Behind the Happy Family Facade*

*Dysfunctional Families:
Healing from the Legacy of Toxic Parents*

The Box of Daughter & Other Poems

What's Your Story? – A Quick Guide to Writing Your Memoir

*Lyme Disease in Remission:
Health Secrets of a 15-Year Veteran*

To Emma, who taught me how to love, and how to love myself.
Thank you for seeing beyond all my problems and faults,
and showing me the beauty of my soul

With special thanks and blessings to Kya

I think I could turn and live with animals,

They are so placid and self-contained,

I stand and look at them long and long,

They do not sweat and whine about their condition,

They do not lie awake in the dark and weep for their sins...

—Walt Whitman, *Leaves of Grass*

Contents

Prologue

The late afternoon sunlight slanted through the branches, weaving lacy patterns of light and shadow on my bedroom wall. Emma lay stretched out on her blanket, paws kneading, tiny pink nose nuzzling the soft mound of blanket she'd formed. Purring loudly, she created an aura of bliss around her as she recreated the kittenhood experience of drinking in life from the cosmos as she nursed.

From the time Emma and I began living together in 1998, she re-enacted this scene of nursing at her mother's breast several times a day, every year, between October and April. I never knew whether she was weaned too early, or whether this was just her personal way of self-soothing.

In later years, she would come crying to my home office, gathering me up with her sweet meow to go to her blanket with her and share our ritual. I would lie with her, arms around her, humming as she purred, drinking in the bliss-energy she created with her simulated nursing. I could feel the love flowing from her, from me, between us, and through the whole room as I imagined myself to be a sister kitten, lying alongside her, enveloped in the softness of mama's fur and the snuggly, purring little bodies all around me.

All of the sadness, anger, and anguish of my life dissolved in the nourishing light of the unconditional love of the Universe and my beloved kitty Emma. She was God in a small, furry package: affectionate, nonjudgmental, never holding a grudge, always offering her love whenever I needed comfort. Emma was a healer who came into my life at just the right time and taught me how to live life with an open heart, to love and be loved without reservation. Not only did she heal my heart, she showed me who I really am, and opened my mind to a much deeper spiritual relationship with the Universe. I am eternally grateful to her.

Chapter 1: Who's in the Dresser?

The first time I saw Emma, I was heading up the front steps to my apartment, and I noticed a sweet little face poking out between the curtains in the apartment next door. A small, gray tabby head with thin black stripes and a perfectly white chin and chest blinked its beautiful green eyes in my direction. We stared at each other for a few moments before she disappeared behind the curtains with a whoosh, like a diva after a curtain call.

I felt like I was in a time warp. Eight months earlier, I had lost Skippy, my beloved gray tabby, to cancer, and the loss of a beloved pet had prompted my move to this new living space. I'd nursed Skippy for four months after her diagnosis, hoping against hope that the combination of traditional and alternative medicine I'd chosen would heal her.

I know many people would have put a pet down at the first cancer diagnosis, but Skippy had been with me through a tough divorce and some difficult years. Our bond was strong, and I wasn't ready to give her up so easily.

During most of her illness, she still enjoyed sitting in the sun and sharing affection with me. But in her last days, I knew the time had come to put an end to her suffering, and I took her to the vet.

I believe in reincarnation, and the thought had crossed my mind that perhaps our beloved animal friends might come back to be with us, in the same way we might have several lifetimes with the same group of souls. After Skippy's death, I had called

Pam, an animal communicator, to see if I could "talk" with Skippy.

"She's very happy to be free and out of her body," Pam said at one point.

"I'm so glad she's not suffering."

"She doesn't want you to suffer, either. She adored you, you know."

I had to swallow before I could speak. "Do you think animals return in new incarnations?" I held my breath, hoping for validation to soothe my heart.

"Absolutely!" Pam replied. "I've talked with many pet owners who are certain a pet has been with them before."

I felt I had to let Skippy know my whereabouts, just in case this weird thing could really happen. "I'm going to be moving to a new space. Is there a sign I could watch for, or something I need to know to find her where I'll be living?"

Pam was silent for a moment. Then she said, "I see a big box of wriggling kittens—all I can see is their tails."

My hope crashed. How would I ever know, out of the hundreds of cats I might see, which one could be Skippy?

"There's one other thing," Pam continued. "Skippy would like to have a more feminine name this time, maybe an 'M' name. She says 'Skippy' didn't really suit her."

I agreed in my mind. Skippy had come to live with me when one of my coworkers noticed that the other cats in his household were ganging up on her. They crowded her when she tried to use the litter box, and she spent most of her time high up on a shelf in the living room to protect herself. When I'd brought her to my apartment, I could see the moment when, sniffing around, she joyfully realized, "There are no other cats here!" She was a beautiful, gentle creature—but I just kept the name she'd been given without a thought.

After Skippy died and I realized I didn't want to stay in the space we'd shared for so many years, I started making plans to move. One night I dreamt that I was going home to my new apartment. The building was a two-story red-brick duplex, long rather than tall, and there were just a couple of steps up to the front door, which was white, set in a white frame. There were two large picture windows on either side of the door—one for each first-floor apartment. In the dream, the building felt like home, and Skippy was sitting on the front steps, as if she was waiting to greet me when I got home.

Weeks later, I was looking at apartments, and one afternoon on the way to see another one, a beautiful sun dog appeared in the sky—a glorious basket of rainbow colors hovering not far above the horizon. As a creative and spiritual person, I often look for "signs" from the Universe, and so I figured the next apartment might be something I'd be interested in.

I pulled into the parking lot, got out of the car, and turned to face the same long, two-story red-brick building with white door and picture windows that I'd seen in my dream. Two steps up to the front door, and I knew this was home. I thanked Skippy for helping me find the apartment of my dreams, and somehow I wasn't too surprised to see a young cat who looked like her peeking out of the window next door a few days after I'd moved in.

The Universe is a marvel! How could I have known what that apartment building looked like before I even saw it? Did Skippy somehow transmit the image to me from the other side? And did my dream mean there could be some kind of connection between Skippy and the young kitty in the apartment next door? I think our animal friends are even more amazing than we already think they are.

Pointed ears standing straight up, the little gray tabby looked directly at me, as if she knew me. I felt as if I was looking at Skippy in a kitten's body, felt a shock of recognition. I took a couple of steps toward her, and the curtains swished shut as she disappeared.

I saw her now and then when I came home. When the curtains were open, an elderly yellow cat could be seen stretched out on the back of the couch in the sun. His ears looked like they'd been injured in a fight, because they were ragged and shortened to within a half-inch of his head, but he always looked blissfully happy.

I began to look forward to sharing a flirting glance or two with the little gray tabby when I came home. Eventually, I could get within a few feet, and we would stare at each other through the glass. I never saw her there when the curtains were open, only when she had the protection of them around her body.

As I developed a peek-a-boo relationship with my neighbor's kitty, I began to think about getting another cat. But the Universe had something else in mind.

One day, one of the other residents mentioned that the woman across the hall from me, who I'd only met a few brief times in the hallway, had been taken off to jail a few days earlier for driving under the influence, and was being held pending investigation of outstanding parking tickets. I thought about the cats in her apartment, and called the landlord to ask if he would check on the cats to make sure they were being fed. A really nice guy, he invited me to have a look to soothe my worries before he hung up.

When he opened the door to the neighbor's apartment, he took one look around and said, "I would rather let the cats go free than leave them here." There were cigarette butts everywhere, and cartons of half-eaten take-out food from days or weeks before had been left on counters and living room tables. Everything was a mess, and the place smelled like a garbage dump.

At least the cats were being fed—there was a huge bag of dry cat food in the center of the kitchen floor, and it had been ripped open so it spilled everywhere. The yellow cat smiled up at us from his place on the sofa, but the small gray tabby was nowhere to be seen.

"Wow," I said. "I've never seen anything like this." My stomach churned as my nose wrinkled at the smell, and my heart broke at seeing animals living in a place like this. I couldn't imagine they were very well cared for if the apartment looked like this.

"I'm gonna call the SPCA," the landlord said. "This isn't right." He pointed at the yellow cat with the stubby ears. "Look at his ears—he had ear mites that were never taken care of."

I thought about Skippy sitting on the steps in my dream, and her resemblance to the beautiful gray tabby who lived here. My throat hurt, and my hands itched to reach for the cats and protect them. I couldn't bear the thought of a sad ending at the SPCA for either of the cats, not to mention the owner's grief at coming home to find them gone. My mind raced to find another solution.

"How about this?" I suggested. "Why don't I take the cats across the hall to my place and take care of them until Sally gets back? I'll leave her a note and let her know that I have them." I held my breath as I waited for the landlord's response.

"That's a great idea," he said. "Anything to get them out of here."

I believe in Providence. It doesn't always act according to our desires, but sometimes synchronicity is so amazing that I have to believe there is some kind of Intelligence in the Universe. Standing in the middle of that apartment, I felt as if the Universe had suddenly dropped a huge gift in my lap. And I had no idea why, because I knew I couldn't keep the cats. I would have to give them back to the owner when she returned.

I scooped up the yellow cat, who began purring loudly and pushing his face into my hand. He was a total lover-boy! The landlord said, "Just close and lock the door when you're done.

I'm gonna come and talk to her when she gets back—this place is filthy." He left, shaking his head, and trotted down the hall stairs as I took the yellow cat across the hall to my apartment and put him on a towel on the sofa.

When I went back for the little tabby, I searched the living room, the kitchen, the bathroom, and the bedroom, trying to ignore the mess. I looked in closets and cabinets, expecting to discover a small tabby face behind each door. Nothing. I checked under the bed—still no sign of her. Remembering Skippy, I checked every high shelf. I checked behind all the curtains. I couldn't find her anywhere. Could she have escaped when we came in?

I was in the kitchen when I heard a soft "thump" from the bedroom. As I walked slowly in, I noticed that one of the dresser drawers was open, clothes spilling out. As I stepped closer, I heard another soft thump at the back of the dresser. I bent to gently pull the drawer out, and the little tabby streaked across the floor and disappeared into the bathroom.

Moving slowly and crooning softly, I went into the bathroom and shut the door. I checked the corners, the bathtub, the closet—nothing. The only hiding place left was the cabinet under the sink. The door was closed, but it hung slightly off the hinges. I carefully opened it, and there, huddled way at the back of the cabinet, was the little gray tabby, scrunched painfully into the corner, with a miserable look on her face that clearly said, "Please don't hurt me." Apparently she had opened the cabinet door, got inside, and let the spring-loaded hinge shut it behind her. I wondered why she was so good at hiding, and why she was so afraid.

I knew just what it was like to feel so terribly frightened, to think the world could come crashing down at any moment, so I wanted to be as gentle and nonthreatening as I could be with her. A memory of huddling on my bed as a child the first time I witnessed my father beating my brother flashed in front of my eyes, and I blinked it away. I felt an almost instant bond with this little kitty. Huddled into the back corner of the cabinet, staring at me with fear and sadness, she roused my caretaking instincts to the highest degree. I felt so sorry for her.

I slowly held my hand out to her so she could sniff my fingers. She pulled back. I gently shut the cabinet door and left the bathroom, shutting the door behind me. Back in my apartment, I went to my fridge and pulled out some deli turkey. She was obviously either a feral cat, or had been mistreated in some way. I instinctively knew I had to make friends with her before I uprooted her from her home, so it didn't seem to her that I was continuing whatever difficulties she'd already had with humans.

I hummed softly as I walked back into my neighbor's apartment. When I held out the turkey, the little tabby flinched, and then her eyes opened wide as she smelled it. After a quick look at me, she gobbled it down. Another piece, another look, more gobbling. All the time, I was crooning softly. Eventually her body began to relax a bit, and I sat down in front of the cabinet to help her get used to my presence.

After awhile, the turkey had a soporific effect, and her eyes began to blink sleepily. Though I wanted to give her more time before I dragged her out from the cabinet, I didn't want to spook her again and lose the chance to get her over to my apartment. To my surprise, when I put my hands around her and began gently pulling her out, she just went limp, as if she knew when she was conquered. I wondered if she'd been passed around from hand to hand during the noisy parties I'd heard across the hall. I gathered her to my heart, nudged the cabinet door shut, and left, locking the door behind me.

When I got to my apartment, I went into the bedroom and pulled out the bottom dresser drawer, removing all the clothes except for a soft sweatshirt, then I set her down in front of it. She raced under the bed. I slid one of the closet doors open just enough for her to get through, in case she needed another hiding place. With all my heart, I wanted to help her feel safe and protected here, to give her the safety I'd never had as a child. I wanted to give her the space to begin feeling cared for and comfortable with life in ways that I'd never had the opportunity to experience myself.

I went into the bathroom, cleared out one of the cabinets, and propped the door slightly open. The yellow cat was still lounging on the towel, apparently happy to just be lying down. He was obviously quite elderly, but seemed content, offering me the sweet love-blinks that cats give to humans. I wondered why the two cats were so very different in their responses to people.

It took less than 24 hours for me to discover that the yellow cat was blind, probably because of the ear-mite infestation. My apartment was a mirror image of my neighbor's across the hall, and the poor cat couldn't figure out where the litter box and the food dish were because everything was backwards.

I watched as the little gray tabby went to the food dish and meowed, over and over, until the yellow cat found the food. Then they ate together. Afterwards, she went to the litter box in the bathroom and meowed, and the yellow cat went to do his business. I was overcome with the knowledge that in spite of her fear, she knew he couldn't see, and she took on the responsibility for showing him where everything was. Later, I found them curled up together on the couch, the yellow cat happily washing the gray tabby, her face and body completely relaxed in total bliss.

I'd left a note for the neighbor to let her know that I had the cats, and two days later she knocked on my door. I didn't know her very well, since I was new to the building. I invited her in, and we sat on the couch talking cats.

"I've had Max since I was eight," she told me, as she sat next to him, petting his ears with obvious affection. "I love him so much, but he's getting old. I wanted him to have comfort in the last part of his life. And I got Emma because I thought Max was lonely—I thought he would like to have a younger cat to perk him up." Her eyes began to fill with tears. "But I think she wears him out. She wants to play, and he just wants to lie in the sun and snooze."

My eyes ran over Sally's unkempt appearance as I thought about her apartment, and I wondered what had happened in her childhood to encourage her to live the way she did. I'm always interested in the backstories of cats and people, always wondering what makes them tick. In spite of my belief that no one should allow their cats to live in such a grubby environment, my heart went out to Sally, just as it had to her kitties.

"I know how you feel," I said. I told her about Skippy. "It's hard to have a cat for so many years, and watch them grow old or get sick."

"Yes," she said. "I'm just not sure it was the right thing to get a cat so young."

I got up and pulled out a small photo album I had made as part of my grieving process after Skippy's death, and showed it to her.

"Emma really looks like the cat I had in New York. Her name was Skippy."

She tilted her head and peered at the photo. "Yes, she does. A little smaller, but the same face and eyes and body shape."

I pulled in a breath, not sure about my next words but unable to hold them back. "If you ever decide you'd rather not have Emma bothering Max, I would be more than happy to take her. I've really missed having a cat."

Sally looked up at me, as if trying to decide whether she could trust me. Her hand stilled on Max's head, and she looked down at the photo again. "Maybe that would be a good idea," she finally said.

My heart soared. Did she really mean I could keep Emma?

Sally began to stroke Max's head again as she confirmed my thought that Emma might be feral. "She was a barn cat," she said. "I got her from a local farm." Then she carefully gathered Max into her arms and stood. "Thanks for taking care of them. I appreciate it." Cradling Max, she nodded her head, and turned toward the door. She seemed to let go of Emma so easily. I wondered whether her decision was made for Max's benefit, or whether Emma's youth and tendency to run and play and claw her way up the curtains had gotten on her nerves.

Feeling like I had to give her an out, I said, "If you change your mind, let me know. After all, she's been your cat for quite awhile now." After just two days, I'd already fallen in love, and I knew it would break my heart to give Emma back, but I had to leave the option open, to be fair. I never heard back from my neighbor, and she moved not too long after that.

My breath caught in my chest as I closed the door behind Sally. Here was the thing I most wanted, presented to me like a gift. As odd as this situation was, everything about it felt right somehow. It made total sense to me, given that I'd had the dream of Skippy on the front steps of the building.

Emma and I began very slowly to forge a loving, affectionate bond. It didn't take me long to realize that "Emma" was a suitably flirty, feminine name—and when I realized that although it didn't begin with an "M," it could certainly fall into the category of an "M" name, I was awed once again by the synchronicity in the Universe.

I finally had myself a cat, and she was the spitting image of Skippy. My grieving heart began to heal.

Over the next 17 years, my relationship with Emma healed more than my heart: after my emotionally abusive childhood, Emma helped me learn that I was lovable, and that I could love, deeply and devotedly. As I healed from issues that had been with me for my entire life, Emma's love offered me the opportunity to dive more deeply into my lifelong journey of self-discovery.

Chapter 2: Life as a Cat

Growing up, there hadn't been much love in my family. My parents had been raised during the Depression and were very religious, so there was a lot of talk about how God is love, and that we should love our neighbors as ourselves, but there was no *feeling* of love in our family. The overall atmosphere was one of struggling and suffering: working too hard, frantically trying to cope, and striving to manipulate life and each other in order to achieve some feeling of control over what was happening. To a child, it felt like constant chaos.

As the youngest in the family, I was the one that everyone practiced their control issues on. I could be controlled; I was smaller, weaker, less knowledgeable by virtue of being younger, and thus easy to control. I was constantly being told, "Do this...Do that...No, don't do it that way, do it this way..." Basically, I was taught that I didn't know how to do anything right, and even when I managed to do something the way my parents wanted, I still didn't please them. They still didn't love or appreciate me—probably because of their own early experiences. So I grew up thinking that there was something very wrong with me, and that I was a deeply defective human being.

My father's father had been a poor minister, and my father's mother had lost a daughter to diphtheria before my father was born. The story goes that she was given a set of lovely plates to decorate after losing her daughter, to help her cope with her grief. My father was grim, gruff, very passive, and not at all affectionate, and as an adult, I began to wonder if perhaps my father had never been able to develop a bond with either of his parents.

My mother had been "the odd man out," as she put it, in her family. She called herself a rebel, and said that her mother had told her she should have been a boy. Her mother apparently treated her two older sisters well, but used my mother as a scapegoat for her anger. So even though my parents may never have discussed it, I believe that part of what drew them together was the depth of unexpressed grief that they both seemed to have. I felt their pain as a child, and tried my best to "love it away," but with little success.

I can't blame my parents for the way they raised me, because I imagine they were raised in a similar way. But that understanding alone doesn't undo all of the emotional damage that had been done.

Though I never felt much love from my mother, she loved cats as much as I did, so I know she was capable of love. Cats were where the love hid in our family. We could shower them with love even though it wasn't safe to love each other, and the cats naturally returned our love unconditionally. If we hadn't had cats, I don't think I would have ever known what love is.

I've always loved cats with a deep and devoted passion. When I was young, we always had a cat or two in the house, and they were always enjoyed and adored. Through caring for cats, I developed a deep connection with and respect for all creatures.

I wrote in my memoir *The Box of Daughter* about the emotional abuse that percolated throughout my childhood and into adulthood. According to my mother, her two older sisters had stuck together and apparently did everything they could to make her feel unwelcome. Consequently, as the only daughter in the family, I was the target of her need to compete with the fairer sex, and since she was bigger this time, she put me down every chance she got.

At heart, my mother was a good woman, and did a lot of good for others with her volunteering. I'm sure she loved me in her own way. But we were very different, and never developed much of a mother-child bond. My father was also emotionally unavailable, and there were no other adults with whom I had regular contact—my grandmothers lived in other states, and my grandfathers were gone by the time I was born.

So, like the baby monkeys who bonded with fur-covered wire monkeys when a mother wasn't available, I bonded with cats instead of humans.

I always felt that cats represented my inner self: the domesticated wildness, innate hedonism, and insatiable curiosity that I instinctively felt was "me" under all the civilizing influences I grew up with. As a child, I identified my inner self at least as much with cats' personalities and behaviors as with human ones. For most of my life, I thought I was odd to have developed this bond with cats, and not have much of a bond with people, but over the years I discovered that many other people have a similar inexpressible attachment to their pets.

I often wonder if people who bond deeply with animals take on some of their characteristics, the way children sometimes reflect facets of their parents' personalities. Do pet owners become like their pets?

During the years I spent in therapy, working to recover from childhood issues, I discovered that the reason I'd never had much of a connection with people stemmed from my lack of attachment to my mother. When babies can't attach to a mother-figure (of either sex), they don't learn how to form a bond with other people. My recovery from the abuse and neglect included learning how to form healthy attachments with others, but even then, my primary bond was still with cats.

One of my favorite memories involves a lovely, elegant black-and-white cat who showed up in our yard in the fall one year when I was eight or nine. We'd lost two cats the previous year— one, an old yellow tom named Tony, who died of old age, and the other, a beautiful gray tabby named Muffin, who had contracted distemper when we boarded her while we went on vacation. So we were catless.

The black-and-white cat came back to our yard every day, pleading with her beautiful eyes for a morsel of food. I begged my mother to let me feed her, and since my mother loved cats, she relented. As it got colder, we allowed the cat to stay in the garage on cold nights.

A few years before, for some reason that I can't remember, my parents had started calling me "Princess." Deep within me, I had always I felt like I should be a princess. In the midst of the rigidity, misery, and fear that seemed to permeate my childhood, I saw myself as a beautiful, confident princess, being loved by all, strong and compassionate and giving in every way. I couldn't understand how I could feel like one thing, and be living in a situation that seemed totally opposite. It still doesn't make sense to me. But in any case, I decided to name the cat "Princess" because she was so elegant.

After a few weeks, we realized that Princess wasn't going to go back to her home, so we adopted her. Once the decision had been made, my mother, ever efficient, took her to the vet for a checkup, and came home to announce that Princess was pregnant. In our family, once a decision was made, it was set in concrete. There was no going back—minds did not change once they were made up.

Princess quickly made herself at home, and grew fatter every day. My mother set up a nice nest for her in a hallway closet, with soft towels and a water dish, but Princess began spending a lot of time in my closet, so we moved the towels there, and one night my mother woke me up after I'd gone to sleep, and whispered, "Princess is having her kittens. Do you want to see?"

"Yes!" I said, and bounded out of bed.

"Quietly," my mother said, as she often did, putting a strong hand on my arm. "Move gently. We don't want to scare them." She had a flashlight so we wouldn't have to turn the lights on, and together we sat down on the floor, side by side, to watch the amazing process of a cat giving birth. It was one of the few times

I felt like I was totally on the same page as my mother—one of the few experiences we both thoroughly enjoyed—and I'm truly grateful to her for waking me and giving me that experience.

I named the kittens Eenie, Meenie, Miney, Mo, and Dearie. Eenie, Meenie, Miney, and Mo were strong, high-spirited black-and-white kittens. Dearie, who was the last one born, was all black except for a white spot on her chest—and the runt of the litter. She often sat and watched the other kittens romp with each other rather than joining in, and would usually wait for them to finish eating before she approached the dish. For several weeks, we enjoyed the antics of the kittens, until the time came when my mother said, "We can't keep all of them. Choose one."

An unceasing champion of the underdog (because I felt like one myself), I chose Dearie. She seemed to reflect the way I felt: unsure of myself, frightened of everyone around me, and left out. Looking back, I realize that I needed to find a reflection of myself somewhere in the midst of the chaos of our family, so Dearie and I—the runts of our families—became best friends. I was away at school when my mother took the other kittens to the shelter, and at that time, I had no idea what often happens at shelters. I suppose my mother knew, and I'm very grateful that she kept it to herself.

Then there was Francis, a very affectionate yellow tabby, who we got several years later from a family in the neighborhood who were moving. Francis had apparently been damaged in some way, and lacked the coordination that most cats have—he would jump up to land on a chair, and slide right into the back of it. He walked across a room with a sort of jaunty, swaying gait, his head bobbling as if it might fall off his body at any time.

Francis let me dress him up in doll clothes, and would happily lie on my bed in a white cotton doll dress, knitted booties, and a pink baby cap tied under his chin, squeezing his eyes open and shut as if he were just the happiest cat in the world.

As a child, I learned early on that when I needed love, I wouldn't get it from my parents. Since both of them had had difficult childhoods, with mothers who were aloof and most likely couldn't bond deeply with them, I imagine they didn't really know how to express love. So when I needed love, I went to our cats. They mirrored back to me the aspects of myself that needed love, affection, and esteem.

I often thought I would have been much happier if I'd been born a cat instead of a person.

I loved all the cats we had, and they offered their unconditional love back to me. Without cats, I believe I never would have known how it felt to have another being respond to me with devotion and affection.

And in my relationship with Emma, I gained a much deeper experience of what it was like to feel loved. When I came home from work, she was always at the door to greet me, rubbing against my legs, purring, looking up at me and offering her head for a love pat. I can still hear her sweet meow as she pushed her face into my hand, as if she was petting me with her head just as I was petting her head with my hand. And I can still see her bounding out of the bedroom to greet me with her beautiful eyes every time I walked in the door, excited simply by my presence.

The experience of having another being always there for me was new to me. I'd had so much experience with people who had their own agendas—who only wanted to get their own needs met, and had little concern for mine. Emma seemed to know when I really needed comfort, and was most affectionate when I needed her affection most. It amazes me sometimes how perfectly our animal companions can read our moods, and how eager they are to help us in any way then can.

Emma also taught me about boundaries, about learning to respect another creature's wishes. Throughout our 17 years together, she never sat on my lap, no matter how often I invited her (though she would occasionally snuggle close to me if it was cold). When I sat down to read or watch TV, if she jumped up on the sofa next to me, I would gently pat my lap, or place her front legs on my lap, or pet her head in the direction of my lap, or even try to move my lap so it was under her—all to no avail. Daintily but firmly, she would back away and lie down next to me. She did let me lift the front half of her body, but she didn't want her front paws on my lap. And as soon as I tried to lift her, she froze and scrambled away.

During the first years of our relationship, I tried occasionally to pick her up for a hug, but she would have none of it—her body immediately stiffened, claws extending. Though she never tried to scratch me, I could sense her terror about being picked up. Eventually I stopped trying to make her do things my way, and came to accept that she would get close in her own way. I began to understand that every creature, and every person, has a certain comfort level with closeness and distance—something I never learned in my family because we were so enmeshed that there were no boundaries at all. We all acted as if we were one single person: my mother. I never learned how to be a separate person. But with Emma, I learned to respect another's boundaries, and to begin developing my own with other people.

Since I had felt so disrespected as a child, I was very careful to respect the way Emma wanted to be treated. I even left the dresser drawer open so she could climb inside when she wanted to, and she often did. For the seventeen years we were together, that drawer stayed open, claimed by Emma as her home-within-our-home. I tried my best to give Emma what she needed. And she did a wonderful job of providing what I needed.

As I was learning to understand and respect another being's needs and boundaries—to allow her to choose how she wanted to be treated, to be loved—I realized I needed to learn how to accept and respect my own needs with the same regard—a difficult task because my parents never had.

Over time, Emma began teaching me how to love myself in the same way that I loved her, and to pay attention to my own boundaries and needs the way I respected the boundaries of others. And over time, I finally began to believe that if such a beautiful, affectionate, perfect creature could love me, then I must be worthy of being loved.

Chapter 3: Mother, Child, Self

Over the next few weeks, as Emma became more accustomed to her new owner and living space, she got a little more curious about what was beyond the front door. I imagine she could still smell her friend, the yellow cat, and I began to feel a little bad about separating them so abruptly. So one morning as Emma squatted next to the front door, sniffing the bit of air that flowed out from under it, I went over and opened the door a crack. She peered out, and when I opened the door wide enough for her to go through, she looked up at me as if to ask if she could go out, then crept into the hallway, eyes focused on the door across the hall.

I went to the window to check the parking lot—I didn't want my neighbor bursting out of her door and frightening Emma. Her car was gone. I went back to the front door and watched as Emma tiptoed up to my neighbor's door and sniffed. She huddled there for a few moments before turning tail and racing back into my apartment. Thereafter, she asked to go out into the hall every few days.

One day when I opened the door, she trotted down the six stairs to the building's front door instead of going across the hall. I figured that if she had truly been a barn cat, she probably had an urge to be outside, as I suppose any animal who was raised in the freedom of the outdoors might have. So the next time I went shopping, I got a leash, and every now and then when Emma headed down the hallway's front steps, I would carefully put the leash on and lead her outside. If I'd lived in the country, I might have let her outside without the leash, but I wanted to train her for living in the city.

After the first few outside visits, she didn't mind the leash because she discovered that putting it on led to all kinds of exciting adventures among the bushes in the building's front yard. Each time she tried to step out into the parking lot, I drew her back to let her know that being on pavement wasn't a good idea. Years later, when I had moved to a house in a quiet neighborhood, I let her outside without the leash, and to my knowledge, she never crossed pavement—she ran along the edge of the road, but didn't set foot on it.

Emma loved sniffing around under the evergreen bushes in front of the apartment building, digging her paws into the cool, soft earth and enjoying the breeze ruffling her fur. Sometimes she went so far into the bushes that I had to let go of the leash and watch it inch along, following her path behind the bushes. Always, when a car turned into the parking lot 200 yards away, she would turn and run for the front door, leash bouncing behind, and I would race her there to get it open for her before people got out of the car and came her way. I imagine that in her mind, my apartment had become the barn of her kittenhood—the safe place to retreat to when danger threatened.

I never discovered the reason for Emma's very unsociable personality. She didn't seem to want to have anything to do with other people, or other cats besides her friend Max—I tried three times over the first ten years we were together to get another cat to keep her company, but all she did each time was hide under the dresser and give up the entire apartment to the other cats, which didn't seem fair, since she had been the first to move in. I finally decided that she liked her space, just like I did, and wanted me all to herself. And I think the fact that she was quite scared of people kept her safe, because she was constantly on the lookout for danger.

By the time I purchased a small house several miles away, Emma was quite used to being outside. Once we'd moved in and she felt comfortable enough to come out of her dresser drawer, I took her outside into the backyard on the leash for the first time. I can still see her sitting on the back porch—where she'd stopped as soon as we went out—staring at the expanse of fenced-in yard before her, with all kinds of bushes, trees, flowers, and plants to explore, taking tentative steps in one direction, then another. Slowly we made our way around the yard, her little pink nose wiggling a mile a minute. The next time I let her out, I left the leash off, leaving her collar and ID tags on, and sat on the porch watching her explore. I loved seeing her enjoy her freedom, and she always came home with plenty to tell me.

During that time I was acting as long-distance caregiver for my parents, who were in their 80s—a difficult process for me. As an only daughter, they had always expected me to cater to them, to pay them loving attention, and to provide for their emotional needs, without giving much in return. I don't know how this pattern got set up in our family, though I suspect that some of it came about because my parents were mismatched enough that they couldn't really meet each other's needs—and though they both believed in giving to the church, or giving help to strangers when they needed it, the pattern behind the closed doors of our family was one of manipulating and maneuvering to get their own needs met (Martha Beck called this form of love "Spider Love" in her wonderful book, *Steering by Starlight*).

In my parents' later years, their habit of expecting me to listen to them and offer support and encouragement increased, and they sometimes called five or six times a day. I felt very drained by both of them, and I relished the idea of Emma being free to come and go as she pleased. Occasionally when I was on the phone with one of my parents, I would catch sight of Emma out in the yard, and imagine how enjoyable and fulfilling it was for her to have complete freedom to be outdoors, unaccountable to anyone but herself.

Though I desperately wanted the same freedom for myself during that time in my life, I could only experience it vicariously through Emma. I even wished I could have an adult-sized dresser drawer to climb into and hide from the world.

I thought about installing a pet door so Emma could come and go as she pleased, but instead I decided to prop the screen door open, open the inside door a crack, and connect it to the doorframe with a bungee cord. She quickly learned that she could get in with a little push on the door—then it swung shut again after she went through it. But she couldn't get out without my help, so while I was at work, I closed and locked the door, and knew she was safe inside.

There was a six-foot rock wall on one side of the house, and one day when I was getting ready to leave for work and went out to the yard to call Emma, I was astounded to watch her bound down the wall, stepping on the little ledges between the rocks, sure-footed and smiling as only cats can smile. I loved thinking of her roaming free, doing whatever she pleased. I don't think she ever went through more than a couple of neighbor's yards, and she almost always came when I called her (at least after she learned that she could get a couple of bites of deli turkey if she came when I called).

Each time she returned home, she greeted me like a long-lost friend, meowing about her adventures, loving me up. She would pop in the door, eyes bright with excitement, tail flipping back and forth as if it was dancing. Sometimes she would wind herself around my legs or a piece of furniture as if she was drawing me a picture of her experiences. I knew it was possible that I might lose her because I let her go out, but her freedom seemed so important to her that I wanted to give her that blessing.

Since I had grown up in what felt to me like a tightly closed, airless, rigid environment, I felt it was unfair to decide how another being might choose to live their life, and I wanted Emma to have the natural freedom that animals are born for. There were few cars in our neighborhood, and it was densely populated, so there wasn't much chance she would become a wild animal's prey. I didn't want her to get to the end of her life feeling like she'd spent her whole life in a box or a cage, the way I had.

One of my fondest memories is the day Emma caught a chipmunk on the rock wall, and ran over to the back door with the chipmunk in her mouth. I was working in the backyard, and saw the chipmunk grab onto the doorframe and hang on for dear life. Emma pushed at the bungee-cord door, and it swung open a few inches, then shut again in her face as the chipmunk held its grip. I rushed over, shouting, "No, Emma! Let it go!", and reached the back porch steps at just the moment the chipmunk let go and Emma pushed on the door and rushed inside with it in her mouth.

I got in the door just in time to see Emma racing up the steps to the second floor, the chipmunk squeaking its little heart out. I ran up the steps and into the bedroom, where I saw Emma sitting in the middle of the floor with a bored look on her face. The chipmunk was nowhere to be seen. I guess Emma figured that since she'd delivered the day's food, her job was done.

I looked under the bed, in the closet, and in all the hidey-holes I could think of, but no chipmunk was to be found. I hoped it was uninjured. Finally Emma wandered over to the corner of the room where the two vents of the heating system merged, sniffed around, and poked her paw into the opening in the usual kitty paw-poking manner. Aha! Chipmunk found.

I went into my office across the hall and called Emma. She came trotting in, and after a few minutes of petting and praising her for contributing to the family's food supply, I went out and shut the door behind me, stopping in the hallway long enough to get a broom from the closet.

Back in the bedroom with broom in hand, after shutting the door I opened the door to the balcony, figuring I could just "sweep" the chipmunk out to freedom. I poked around in the heating vent, causing a series of chirps and thumps, and finally ended up taking the covers off the vents. The chipmunk cowered in the corner. To my relief, I didn't see any blood or strangely shaped body parts. Everything looked normal.

Speaking softly, I told the chipmunk that there was an open door ten feet away, and if it would just head in that direction, it would be free. Moving the broom slowly, slowly around behind it, I swished the broom against the wall, hoping the chippie would startle at the noise and head for freedom. The poor thing just stared up at me with a look of terror on its furry face. So I bumped the broom gently against its backside, and off it raced— right past the open door and under the dresser!

It took seven back-and-forth crossings of the room before I got the chipmunk to go out the door. Life with animals would be so much easier if we could speak each other's languages! But I suppose that's part of the mystery of life. If we could talk to the animals the same way we talk to other human beings, I'm afraid we'd create similar kinds of dysfunction in our relationships.

When I opened the door to the office, Emma was lazing languidly in the sun—one of her favorite spots. She didn't even lift her head to ask what had happened with the chipmunk. She probably already knew.

In the book *Between Pets and People: The Importance of Animal Companionship* by Alan Beck and Aaron Katcher, the authors suggest that pets can represent to their owners a loving mother, a devoted child, and even the self. In my case, Emma was every one of these.

Emma provided a real sense of stability in my life when it seemed like everything else reflected the chaos of my childhood— she was always there when I got home, and when I got up in the morning—and her presence always grounded me. Emma provided a sense of constancy in my life, which I'd never experienced, for the 17 years we were together.

Because I was never taught that I was loving or lovable when I was a child, I grew up believing that cats were loving and lovable, but that I was not. Though I'd been married and divorced, and had many friends and acquaintances, Emma represented the only true experience of consistently feeling loved over the long term that I'd had in my entire life.

Receiving and sharing love with animals has always felt so much safer to me than risking my heart with human relationships, because the love I experienced in relationship with my parents almost always had hurt attached. As a result, I seem to have grown up identifying more with cats than with the world of humans—which actually makes sense to me as an adult, because there seems to be so much craziness, dysfunction, and lack of compassion in a large portion of the human race.

I'd never had a bond with an animal where I felt we were like "sisters under the skin"—alike in so many ways. I saw so much of myself reflected in Emma. We both preferred privacy to lots of socializing; we both felt more comfortable in a quiet, natural environment; we both liked to have space around us; and neither of us enjoyed someone else providing a lot of close body contact, unless we were in the mood. I often wondered whether we just happened to be a great personality match, or whether we began to reflect each other in the same way that humans who move in together sometimes do.

I realize now that Emma represented the most tender, loving, affectionate, and vulnerable part of me—the deepest part of myself. Though I had never wanted children, I'd always loved "mothering" the cats I lived with, caring for their every need, petting and loving them, and generally treating them all like princesses. Years after Emma came into my life, I realized I had projected my own vulnerable self onto cats when I was very small, as if I was "storing it" in the cats I mothered so that that part of me was never totally lost, and I could vicariously experience being loved and appreciated.

Since my parents were so wrapped up in their own needs, they couldn't really mirror me as a child—and I imagine that I unconsciously chose cats as my mirror, perceiving them to be the perfect, loving, beautiful beings I would have been if I was "normal" rather than "defective." By taking care of, loving, and petting cats, I had found a way to take care of, love, and nurture myself.

As young as I was, some part of my psyche knew that I had to stash my real self away so that I didn't completely "disappear" in response to repeated rejection and turn into a human robot. And over the years of my recovery, I have reclaimed that real self, bit by bit and piece by piece, until I feel much more whole and much more real.

Emma helped me learn what it might've been like to have a loving, attentive mother—happily greeting me when I got home, waking me with love in the morning, giving comfort when I'd had a bad day—just by being present to me. She gave me a loving foundation which helped me learn how to love myself.

I wonder sometimes if our relationships with our pets reflect the true beauty and loving nature of our souls, whereas our interactions with people reflect the personalities we've developed in response to how we were brought up and our reaction to the society in which we live. I always seem to feel completely free to be myself with animals, but no matter how much I've tried, I always wear some part of my social mask when I'm with people. That habit is just too deeply ingrained.

I think I am more like a cat than a person. Perhaps that's the result of the abuse I experienced—as if my childhood dug a hole deep inside of me which was never filled. As a child, I wanted to be as free and uninhibited and truly myself as cats are, and to be loved for that rather than for how much attention I paid to someone.

I wonder if this is how we're supposed to exist in the world. Perhaps we're so attached to our pets because they remind us of the purity of heart and the beauty of soul that we all possess.

Since I identified so deeply with cats in childhood, my "role models" in childhood were an uneasy blend of my parents' rigidity, self-denigration, and dysfunctional ways of relating— which instilled in me the "shoulds" and "have-tos" of civilized life—and the free and unconditionally loving way of being that cats represented to me, along with their complete self-integrity and freedom to express themselves just as they are. So I often feel like I'm a two-headed person occupying two different worlds—a much better match for the world of nature than the practical human world.

Cats express themselves totally freely, are totally nonjudgmental of others, and seem to be in touch with all of life, undeterred by people who don't care for cats, and uncaring about their own or others' missteps. This is who I feel myself to be on the deepest level, and I wonder if it's how human beings were meant to be. I have trouble coping with the world that humans have created because I feel more like a cat inside than a human, and I view the foibles of the human world with as much head-shaking as I imagine animals do.

I believe that one of the major ills of most societies today is the repression of individual self-expression. Especially in America, we're encouraged not to show our feelings or express our deepest needs. Most of us are reared to go out into the world and make as much money as we can—but what we lose is a strong connection to our humanity and individuality. Some people even lose their souls. At least we can maintain that connection through our pets, and hopefully one day, our society will change so that we're more free to be who we really are.

On some primordial level, my soul finds it almost too painful to cope with what seems like an alien society. It feels as if I don't belong here; as if I'm too light and sweet and vulnerable deep inside to face the hard issues of everyday life: the toil, the pain, the loss, the bombardment of noise and ugliness, and other people's frustration and pain.

I have a hard time relating to most of the human world—the busyness, the competition, the rushing, the desire to get ahead. All I want is to experience the depth and breadth of life, to be the most glorious expression of the soul that I am.

I wonder if children who never get the chance to develop a bond with a human parent live too much from their souls because they never get planted in the physical world, or whether they never develop a strong connection with the Universe because they lacked that original bond with an Other.

In an ideal world, our parents would exemplify God (or the Universe) for us as children, and provide the love and understanding and forgiveness and guidance that God (or the Universe) gives to us as adults. I guess this is why so many religions have teenagers go through a service (such as a baptism or a Bar Mitzvah) where their parents "turn them over to God." As adults, I think we're supposed to know what being loved by God or the Universe is like, because we were supposed to be loved that way by our parents beforehand. Maybe only our animal companions can truly do that.

I'm fully convinced that when a baby doesn't have the opportunity to bond with a person—a mother, father, or other caretaker—and there are animals available, the soul will bond with animals instead of humans. I wonder if this is why some people seem to have such extraordinary bonds with horses, dogs, or cats.

I've never really connected with people during my lifetime, much as I've recovered from my childhood, much as I've tried to connect. I have loved a few people, but as I look back on those relationships, those people were particularly full of the unconditional love and nonjudgment that I associate with animals.

Though I have a deep desire to connect with animals, with nature, and with the Universe, the idea of connecting with people is not so appealing to me, and I think this is a direct result of my development. I imagine this absence of attachment to people stems from the fact that people used me for a large part of my life, and like an animal who has been hurt too many times by a human, I just want to stay away like Emma in her dresser, to hide in my nest and just be with other animals. But humans don't always have that choice.

Chapter 4: Bonding Rituals

After seven years of acting as caregiver for my parents, I was completely drained, and must admit I was relieved when they passed away within a few years of each other. Although Emma thoroughly enjoyed the yard, stone walls, and chipmunks where we lived, I wasn't able to continue upkeep on the old house I had bought. I was just too burned out.

Everywhere I turned, I felt my parents' presence, because their needs had so invaded my life in the house, and I was impatient to move on with my life and grow beyond the emotional and mental box I had grown up in. I needed to recover from the strain of caregiving without the old memories surfacing each time I went into another room. So I started looking for a new place to live.

Each time I went to look at a possible new home, I thought about Emma. Would she be safe going outside? Would she enjoy the new surroundings the way she did now? How could I make the change as easy for her as possible? After looking around for several months, I finally found a place that seemed safe, with a few nice stands of trees where she could hunt chipmunks.

It wasn't 'til after we moved that I discovered there was a problem in the neighborhood with coy dogs—a cross between wolf and dog—and that they liked to eat cats. So I began once again going outside with Emma each time she went out, carrying a flashlight to surprise any offender who came near. I felt sorry for her—for years she'd been used to freely roaming the neighborhood, and now her mom was hanging close by and calling her to come in a scant ten minutes after she'd gone out. But I managed to keep her safe from predators.

And she had street smarts of her own. One day, she sat next to the door, wanting to go out, and when I opened the door and cracked the screen door, she started snuffling and snorting, the hair on her back puffing up to twice its normal size. She turned around and raced back to her dresser drawer—and the next day a neighbor mentioned that a young bear had been sighted a quarter of a mile away.

In the winter when Emma didn't enjoy going out, I attached bird feeders to the windows for her entertainment while I was working. More than once, I saw her bang her paw on the window, sending the birds fluttering, and I thought of how I'd felt as a girl, forced to live in a predetermined and confining role in childhood. Was it more frustrating than enjoyable for her to be able to stand right next to the birds, but not be able to get at them?

And even after we'd been together for years, she still would not sit on my lap, so I never forced her to. I imagine she must have had a bad memory attached to the idea of sitting on a human's lap. Even though she hated my touching her fluffy white tummy, it was so beautiful that I had to touch it, maybe once a year or so, but eventually I stopped doing that as well, in respect of her wishes.

She enjoyed our little rituals, and I did, too—feeding her bits of turkey with my fingers or a bit of coconut oil in my palm, which she asked for by ducking her head and touching her nose to the floor or the bedspread, and the "airplane" rides which became our substitute for lap-sitting.

Emma loved boxes, and whenever there was a file box open in my office, she would plop down in the lid and lie there contentedly, blinking up at me with a happy-kitty smile on her small face. One day, on a whim, I gently picked the box up with her in it, and started making soft airplane noises as I moved around the room, carrying her in the box top. As we went by the window, she craned her neck to look out, so I stopped for a moment while she observed the outside world. Then I continued around the room. She seemed to enjoy it, so I went a little faster. I imagine it was like a carnival ride for a youngster—something new and different, a sense of movement and air flying by a little faster than usual.

In fact, it looked like she enjoyed it so much that I was reluctant to stop, even though my arms were tired. So I sat down with the box on my lap, and started petting her. So far, so good—no jumping down or zooming for the dresser drawer. I rocked the box back and forth with my knees, petting and singing to her, and eventually she laid her head down and went to sleep. So I finally got Emma to sit on my lap. She didn't mind, as long as she was in a box.

This became a regular ritual for us. Sometimes, when she seemed to need attention, I would set the box on the floor beside her, she would climb right in, and off we'd go. I took to leaving the box top on the floor in a corner of my office, and sometimes she would get in, sit down, look up at me, and meow for a ride. How quickly we adapt to the activities our animals love to share with us! I loved the end of the ritual most—gentle petting and soft singing, nourishing both of us with the love that flowed between us. After that, I made sure I always had a good supply of boxes.

Over the next few years, as the economy crashed and burned, I found it harder and harder to make a living. I had to spend more time in my office, more time working away from home, and less time with Emma. She was getting older, needing me more and more as my parents had. Looking back, I realize that I withdrew a little from the closeness of our relationship, and my willingness to take care of all of her needs began to diminish as a result of my own tiredness and stress.

During one of our annual vet visits, the vet discovered that Emma's blood pressure was high, and recommended giving her medication. I'm not a big fan of giving medications to either pets or people, because I believe they disrupt the system in other ways, even while they might fix the problem for which they're prescribed. I asked the vet what would happen if we just let it ride, and she said that strokes were common in animals with high blood pressure. I thought about trying a homeopathic route, but truth to tell, I was so tired and stressed at that point that it felt too overwhelming to start investigating alternative options as I had with Skippy. So we started Emma on the medication.

I'd always been careful with her vaccinations—requesting as few as possible, and never more than one at once—because Skippy's cancer had been diagnosed not too long after I took her to the vet's for a digestive disorder, and while she was there recovering from a bacterial infection, he gave her a couple of vaccinations. According to some holistic vets, cat's systems are even more sensitive than people's, and multiple vaccinations can cause major problems. I didn't consider that a medication might create the same kind of response.

Late in the fall when Emma was seventeen, I noticed a lump in her jaw, and immediately took her to the vet. I assumed it was an impacted tooth, since at her age she'd already had a couple of bad teeth removed. We went home after some tests, and I was devastated a few days later when the results came back. Cancer. Again.

Even though the high-blood-pressure medication had kept Emma alive, I kicked myself for giving it to her. The chemical "fillers" in the medication had probably played some part in the development of her disease.

I asked the vet about painkillers. She responded that there wouldn't be any pain, and I wondered, how do they know? How can they be sure that animals don't experience pain? I asked about surgery, but the tumor had penetrated Emma's jawbone too deeply for that to be an option.

I began to wonder if Emma had sensed my distress over the struggle to make a living, and had felt like I was withdrawing from her when I was too busy. I can't say I neglected her, because

I still took care of her physical needs, and gave her attention and love when I could. But I know that I was often rushed, or thinking I should be getting back to work when I took her on a too-quick airplane ride, sometimes even petting her without joy, just because I thought she needed it. I think pets can sense when our hearts are not totally open, whether they know the reason or not.

At least I did stop what I was doing sometimes when Emma needed attention, and gave her all the attention I could. Sometimes I appreciated the "breaks" from work that she provided. But I'm still bothered because my love for her seemed manufactured after awhile, instead of natural. I don't know why, and I don't know what to do with that feeling. Was it just that we'd been together so long that I took her for granted? Was she more needy as she grew older? Was I just too busy to pay attention to the important things in life? Was I acting on automatic pilot rather than mindfully?

Over time, I realized that the reason I sometimes became irritated with her needs and wanted to ignore them was because I wasn't getting my own needs met—although it certainly wasn't Emma's fault—and that reminded me of my relationship with my mother. I didn't realize that in wanting to ignore Emma's demands, I was also ignoring my own desires for affection, love, and enjoyment.

But animals are completely and totally forgiving—we may sometimes neglect them, or communicate irritation when they demand our attention—but they forgive over and over, and still love us. Each time they come to us, they come anew with unconditional love. Children are the same with their parents, no matter how much they're hurt—they forgive over and over again, and continue to try every day to please these people in hopes of receiving love one day instead of mistreatment.

For people who grew up in emotionally abusive families like I did, loving a pet can be the only way they have to love themselves, and facing the loss of that connection is completely overwhelming.

Most of us are so conditioned from an early age not to acknowledge and express our feelings that sometimes we don't even know that they're there. Living with a pet can offer a marvelous opportunity to maintain contact with the "inner child" aspect of the self—the part of us that still enjoys affection and play and uninhibited self-expression.

By the same token, having a pet can allow us, for better or worse, to let the pet become our *primary* source of that connection to our deepest selves, so that we eventually begin to *identify* that part of ourselves exclusively with the pet. Then if the pet becomes ill, that most divine and human aspect of ourselves may feel extremely threatened—we fear that if we lose the pet, that part of ourselves will be lost as well. This is exactly what I went through with Emma. I felt as if my own life force was diminishing as hers diminished, and I feared I would lose myself altogether when she died.

As I watched her get weaker day by day, I felt like a part of myself was dying, and I didn't know how to stop it. I didn't know how to separate from the bond I had developed with a cherished pet. I felt that I was desperately trying to save a part of myself that had been lost and bewildered for a long time, and I was losing the battle.

It wasn't until later that I understood that in taking care of her, I had also been taking care of the lost child inside of me, giving the attention to Emma that I had craved as a child and not received.

As I watched her in her suffering, totally stoic as cats often are, the bottomless depth of my inner child's suffering during the five decades my parents had abused me came welling to the surface. In Emma's beautiful face, distorted and twisted by the tumor, I saw my own experience of feeling emotionally and mentally deformed as a child—being pulled and pummeled and wrenched into a psychic shape that I no longer recognized as myself.

As I looked under the surface of that image of being defective, which I'd carried with me through most of my life, I began to sense a connection to the beautiful, perfect child I had been before the dynamics of my dysfunctional family warped my self-image—the beautiful, perfect, original self that I saw reflected in Emma, but had lost touch with in myself.

I watched Emma's mouth hanging always slightly, crookedly open, bulging on one side, and I understood how I had had to distort myself into an unnatural and uncomfortable sense of who

I was in order to meet my parents' expectations. As I knelt next to the bed, petting Emma and sharing love-blinks with her, all my feelings of being twisted and misshapen throughout my life bubbled up to the surface.

Yet Emma was still looking at me with love, and I still looked at her with love in spite of her deformity, perhaps even more because I felt so sorry for her in her illness. I'd always compared myself to what I perceived to be the perfection of nature, and had always felt myself to be more like a half-alive flower trying to squeeze itself up through a crack in the sidewalk than a sturdy plant with plenty of nutrients, plenty of sunshine, and plenty of space. But as I looked at Emma in that moment, I realized that I was lovable in spite of my feelings of being deformed and defective.

My parents had always insisted that everything be perfect— that *I* be perfect—and like any family with a strong drama addiction, even a small imperfection, mistake, or mishap elicited a response of horror. And over the years, the juxtaposition of always falling short of being "perfect" in their eyes butting up against the way I felt distorted inside nearly tore me apart, and made me feel even more defective.

I wonder now if the feelings of being defective were caused in part by my inability to use my natural strengths, to do things my own way, since my parents always insisted I follow their orders and methods, and sharply criticized my own efforts to do things my way.

Since I had treated Skippy's cancer years before, I was familiar with a lot of the herbal and homeopathic remedies often used to treat cancer in felines. I tried one after another—each time hoping against hope that this time, I would be able to heal my closest companion. Some of the remedies seemed to slow the progression of the illness, but nothing reversed it. I often wonder if animals, as well as people, just give in to an illness when they're tired enough, or sad enough, to want to stop living.

Even as Emma neared the end of her illness, she still enjoyed sitting in the sun and watching the birds, and I felt no judgment from her about the progress of her disease or the methods I had chosen to treat her. She still enjoyed whatever she could, and accepted what was happening as part of the natural cycle of life, offering no resistance. Watching her helped me to see the little annoyances of my life in a new way, and taught me to focus on what's enjoyable in life—the little rituals of love we share with our pets, ourselves, or other people—rather than on sadness or frustration.

Watching Emma's decline, and thinking back over our years together and how we'd met, I realized that the deepest part of me was so wounded that it felt like a sad, skinny abandoned kitten— the Emma I had found in my neighbor's apartment. I knew I had to start loving and caring for that part of myself with as much attention and love and nourishment as I would give to a real abandoned kitten—to nurse it back to health and strength and happiness. I wasn't sure how to do that, so I started experimenting.

One of the things I'd always loved as a child was doing jigsaw puzzles. So I got a couple of colorful puzzles, and started making time to sit down and "play" with them. As a writer and editor, I am so tied to the computer, to the black-and-white of words and paper or screen, that sitting down to work on a puzzle for a bit offered not only time with my "inner child," but the opportunity to work with color, image, and shape. Puzzles became a welcome break from work, and a way to help my inner child feel as if I was paying attention to her. And every time I got a new puzzle, I could almost hear my inner child saying, "Thank you," with a little anticipation of delight. In those moments, I began learning how to offer her the comfort, nourishment, and love that I had always lavished on cats instead.

On a subconscious level, I knew I had to learn that even though I would always care for my pets very deeply, perhaps even more than any other beings on the planet, I am still the most important being in my life, and deserve as much consideration, attention, and love as I give to my pets. As I coped with the fact that Emma might not be around much longer, I tried to keep reminding myself that I have all the beautiful and lovable qualities that Emma had—and that she was simply reflecting back to me the love I have to offer and the love that I deserve.

It was becoming very clear to me that loving cats had always been a substitute for loving myself, and I could sense how unhealthy that pattern was, in that it kept me from connecting with myself, with others, and with the Universe in a fulfilling way. I wanted to learn to love myself as deeply as I loved Emma—to give myself the same love and concern and support that I gave my beloved friend. I wanted to learn that I could love myself like that for the rest of my life, no matter what, and that the Universe could be there for me in the same way that Emma was.

Chapter 5: Emma's Choice

One unusually warm morning in early February, after spending the winter months completely indoors, Emma slowly padded downstairs and went to her customary "Please let me out" spot. She didn't usually go out in daylight, and I was nervous about letting her out while she was ill, but I was still committed to giving her the freedom to choose what she wanted to do. So I put her collar on, and let her out.

As always, she trotted down the back steps, ran immediately to the small stand of trees not far away, nosed her way in, and sat down right in the middle with her face to the sun.

And as always, I sat down on the deck to keep her safe.

I've read that when animals decide they want to die, they go into the woods and place themselves in the path of predators. I wondered if Emma was offering herself up to be taken—if she had had enough, and was ready to go. I'm just glad that she had one more day in the sun, sitting happily on the earth she loved amidst the rocks and trees, feeling the sun on her face and the breeze ruffling her fur. After awhile, I called her, and she slowly came back.

The vet had told me that Emma would let me know when she wanted to go. As long as she was eating, I assumed she wasn't feeling too bad. But how can we really know? Cats generally don't exhibit signs of discomfort unless they're in considerable distress. In spite of the fact that she needed more care as her illness progressed, I wanted to let her make the decision about when she wanted to go, rather than just deciding myself, and ending her life.

The paradox of taking care of our animal friends as they near the end of their lives is that we love them, but depending on the amount of care we have to give them, we can also begrudge the time and effort we spend. When does the balance tip so that the burden of caring for them becomes heavier than the power of love?

I noticed that she wasn't hiding under the dresser the way she used to—she pretty much stayed on the bed. I wondered if it had become too difficult for her to climb up behind the drawers. So I lined a box with the softest furry material I could find, and placed it on the bed for her to hide in. She immediately claimed it as "home," and spent most of her sleeping and resting time in the box from then on. I still wanted to do everything I could for her, not fully realizing yet that I was also taking care of the tiny part of myself that identified with her.

Throughout our relationship, I had done everything I could to make her comfortable, from leaving the dresser drawer open most of the time, to finding places to move to where she could safely go outside, to abstaining from picking her up and cuddling her close, much as I wanted to, because that was beyond her comfort level. I so wanted to give her the space and freedom to be who she was that I'd wanted as a child. Knowing that I'd given her everything she needed helped me to have compassion for myself in the midst of the resentment I felt.

Over the years, I had often sat down on the floor next to the bed, and cuddled with Emma, my arms in a circle around her body, my face against her fur, humming slightly as she purred at the contact. Feeling part of myself immersed in her, this seemed like the perfect way for both of us to keep our boundaries, yet enjoy the closeness we both craved. One of the most wonderful aspects of a healthy human-animal relationship is how completely we adapt to each other's needs. Because animals so nonjudgmental, there's usually very little of the struggle for dominance and the self-centeredness which sometimes permeates human relationships.

Whenever I thought of it, I told Emma in words and with my mind that she was free to let me know when she wanted to go. I believe that animals know our thoughts—maybe not in English or in any way we can fathom—but I do think they catch our meaning somehow. I still told her I loved her, too.

Sometimes she showed signs of being ready to give up—not finishing a meal, or not coming to greet me when I walked into the room—which made me think she was ready to go, but then she would rally shortly thereafter, or curl up to sleep with one of those lovely contented-kitty smiles, and I would think to myself, "A little while longer, then."

I truly believe that humans and animals communicate on levels we're not at all aware of, and that animals are aware of our feelings and thoughts on a moment-to-moment basis. How else would dogs know ahead of time that their owners are on the way home? I imagine the psychic bond between humans and their pets is similar to the bond between mothers and children that allows mothers to know instinctively when their children are in trouble, or allows us to know when a person we're close to has passed on.

During Emma's last few days, a black cat which I'd occasionally seen before in the neighborhood sat vigil on my deck. When I went out in the morning to sit in the sun, he was curled up there, watching my every move, offering his own version of love-blinks and support. I felt as if he knew somehow that Emma was nearing the end—as if he knew we both needed support and encouragement in our final days together.

Though to my knowledge Emma never actually had contact with the black cat because she was a total introvert with both people and other cats, I'd seen her watching him outside as she sat in front of the window, monitoring his comings and goings with a rabid attention that made me wonder if she wished with all her heart she could make friends in spite of her fear. I felt the same way sometimes in my dealings with people. I'm still amazed by how perfectly our personalities mirrored each other.

I'm sure she must have known the black cat was visiting— perhaps he even gave her some kind of comfort with that innate long-distance communication that all cats seem to have.

The day after Valentine's Day in 2013, after feeding Emma in the morning and heading into my home office to work, I came back into the bedroom around 9am to see how she was doing. She stood up weakly to greet me, but didn't come to the edge of the bed. I noticed that she hadn't eaten anything. I went to the kitchen and brought back some turkey, one of her favorite treats, and offered it in the palm of my hand. She sniffed it, thought about eating, and then turned away. I stood and watched for a moment as she turned back around, sat down, and gave me a look that clearly said, "I don't want to do this anymore."

I sat on the edge of the bed, intent on making sure this was what she was communicating. Not really expecting a clear answer, I still felt compelled to ask her, "Does this mean you want to go now?" She blinked and looked away. I petted her and loved her up for awhile, then went to call the vet to arrange a time to come in that day.

The assistant who answered the phone said, "I'm so sorry. What time would you like to come in? We have an 11am and a 2:30pm."

I hesitated, wanting to put it off as long as possible. "2:30 would be good." After I finished the call, I went back upstairs to be with Emma. She was obviously uncomfortable, and since I know that cats tend not to show their discomfort unless they're truly feeling wretched, I went back down, called the vet again, and asked for 11am. Much as I knew I would suffer after Emma was gone, I didn't want her to suffer in her illness anymore.

On the way to the vet's office, I placed my hand on the screen of Emma's carrier just as I always had when we were going to the vet, because I knew how much she hated going there, and I wanted to comfort her as much as I could. For the first time in all the years and vet visits we'd had, she pushed her face right up against my hand, giving me what I took to be a "thank you" for my help in ending her suffering.

I've wondered since if she somehow knew Valentine's Day was approaching, and chose to wait until it was over before letting me know she was ready to go. It reminded me of the day I met with my father's funeral director to plan the funeral. I told the director that my father had passed the day before my parents' wedding anniversary, and he responded, "You'd be surprised how often that happens." It makes an odd kind of sense to me, given our deep bond, that Emma would wait until the Day of Love had passed before she left my life.

As I think back on that time, I am so very grateful to Emma for giving me a joyful lesson in love that I might never have experienced otherwise. Even as I went through the grieving process, I noticed that my tears were still a mixture of sadness at missing Emma and grief for the loving mother I never had.

That's when I began to believe with all of my being that Emma represented the tiny self from years ago who never got to be a child, and who just wanted to be taken care of without having to drain herself by always paying attention to other people. By taking care of Emma, I could take care of that part of myself, give my tiny self all the comfort, love, and acceptance she wanted. How could I continue to do that after Emma was gone? How could I nurture the part of me deep inside that needed the kind of love she provided?

A few days later, when I had finished scattering Emma's ashes in the garden, the black cat showed up again, and sniffed around the flowers where I had placed her remains. Usually a very enthusiastic head-butter, he was suddenly much more gentle as I stroked him, even displaying a bit of Emma's delicate, elegant movements instead of his usual strutting maleness.

I wondered if somehow her spirit joined him for a few moments, needing a last physical contact with me before she was finally free. He sat with me for awhile, looking out over the yard, peaceful and content, and watching him, I felt an unusual sense of freedom and light, as if scattering her ashes had scattered and dissolved my grief and pain, and now it was okay to be peaceful and content.

I'm looking forward to someday meeting Emma at the Rainbow Bridge, where I hope that my questions about life and love and our profound connections with each other will finally be answered. I offer my heartfelt appreciation to the unknown author of the following piece, which helped me tremendously in my grieving process, gave me hope, and helped me realize that others have the same unfathomably deep bond with pets that I do—and that perhaps I am normal in an abnormal world, instead of abnormal in a normal world.

Rainbow Bridge

Just this side of heaven is a place called Rainbow Bridge.

When an animal dies that has been especially close to someone here, that pet goes to Rainbow Bridge. There are meadows and hills for all of our special friends so they can run and play together. There is plenty of food, water and sunshine, and our friends are warm and comfortable.

All the animals who had been ill and old are restored to health and vigor; those who were hurt or maimed are made whole and strong again, just as we remember them in our dreams of days and times gone by. The animals are happy and content, except for one small thing: they each miss someone very special to them, who had to be left behind.

They all run and play together, but the day comes when one suddenly stops and looks into the distance. Her bright eyes are intent; her eager body quivers. Suddenly she begins to run from the group, flying over the green grass, her legs carrying her faster and faster.

You have been spotted, and when you and your special friend finally meet, you cling together in joyous reunion, never to be parted again. The happy kisses rain upon your face; your hands again caress the beloved head, and you look once more into the trusting eyes of your pet, so long gone from your life but never absent from your heart.

Then you cross Rainbow Bridge together....

—Author unknown

Chapter 6: Soul Retrieval

Over the next few weeks, I began to realize that the extent to which I missed Emma—and I missed her terribly, as if there were a hole in my heart the size of Texas—was the extent to which I needed to learn to love myself. I missed her the way someone else might miss her mother when she passed away, because Emma was my first experience of being loved unconditionally.

In the midst of my misery, I felt as if the Universe was prompting me to ask, "How can I learn to love myself as much as I loved Emma?"

In the days that followed her death, I began to grieve not only the loss of Emma herself, but the loss of the "mother love" that she had represented. Without her presence, it became very clear to me that our bond had been a substitute for the love I'd never experienced with my mother. I began to understand that Emma was a gift in my life, a gift that helped me understand what it's like to be loved. I tried to focus on gratitude for this gift, and it lifted my spirits a little.

My relationship with Emma had kept me from fully realizing the devastation of never having felt loved by my mother. Emma's love provided an affectionate and devoted substitute for the love I had so desperately needed as a child. Though I imagine my mother loved me in her own way, I never felt love coming from her; most of my experiences with my mother had created feelings of not being good enough, of being defective in some way, without knowing how to do better or how to get her to love me.

Emma taught me something I had never known before: that I could be loved, that I was lovable. For the first time in my life, I felt unconditional love from another being all the way to my core. I saw myself reflected with eyes of love.

All of the love in the Universe had been bundled into one small kitty's body—and the rest of life just seemed hurtful and hard. Part of me felt that having a cat was the only way I could give and receive love with the Universe—the only conduit to real love that I'd ever had. But another part of me understood how limiting this perspective can be.

In the days after Emma died, I felt as if my soul had been ripped from me. All the joy, beauty, love, affection, and peace she'd brought to me day in and day out was gone. And I realized that when I'd had to give up my soul as a child in order to take care of my parents emotionally and try please them however I could, I had literally placed my soul into the cats I'd had for safekeeping, so I would never truly lose it.

I wonder if this is what some other devoted pet owners had to do early in life.

As a child, I'd had to cast aside one precious part of myself after another, and some part of me sought a "container" for all of the split-off aspects of myself. Though it's not in my memory, at some point I must have unconsciously chosen cats on which to project all of these disowned parts of myself. I think of it now as "storing" all those aspects of myself in a general cat "personality," staying connected with those disallowed aspects of my self by tucking them safely into cats where no one would think to look for the real me.

I needed to figure out how to retrieve my soul. I knew I could touch in with it in my writing, because my writing is one of my deepest connections with my inner self. I found ways to connect with my soul in nature, wrapping myself in the quiet and splendor of sunlight shining through pine tree branches. But I needed something more.

I needed to open myself to all the love in the Universe, which was a scary idea for me, because when I'd opened myself as a child, I'd experienced criticism and hurt.

But sometimes moving forward into a very frightening unknown becomes preferable to living with the increasing pain you've lived with for so long.

When I mentioned to my landlord that Emma had died, he didn't even say he was sorry. Instead he said, "No more cats!" and posted a notice in the hall to that effect. Apparently, some other cat owner had left a huge mess behind after the cat sprayed all over the apartment. So I was stuck with myself until I could find a new place to live.

I began to realize that the tremendous love I'd given to cats all my life was a way of expressing not only how much *I* needed love, but also how much love I wanted to give. All I'd ever wanted was for someone to care for me the way I'd cared for Emma—to love me for my absolutely natural, real, deepest self, the way I loved her totally natural self. My childhood experience was so far away from that that I wondered if I could even connect with my original self, my soul. As I often do when I'm trying to heal some aspect of my life, I started looking at the situation from every angle I could think of.

I thought about everything that Emma represented to me. She was a very loving and affectionate being, reflecting back to me the love that I shared with her. I saw her as a natural and almost childlike creature, following her whims and being herself, and I wanted that freedom for myself as well. I wanted to be able to totally accept all of myself on that deep a level.

I considered the ways in which I felt Emma and I reflected each other—at times, I had even felt as if Emma was partly me, and I was partly Emma, so that when I cared for her, I was also caring for myself. I wanted to learn how to be all me, and incorporate Emma's best qualities, so I could finally be whole.

As I journeyed deeper into this quest, I eventually realized that Emma represented the "princess" aspect of myself that I'd sublimated decades before. Her beauty, elegance, and confident, unashamed sense of self embodied the self I had thought myself to be as a child, but was shamed for expressing. I needed to try to reclaim those aspects of myself that I had projected onto her, and other cats, in order to save myself from being totally lost in childhood. I wanted to treat myself as gently and care for myself as much as I did for Emma.

I had more success on some days, less on others. Sometimes I fell back into the "work so hard it's like punishing yourself" pattern, but sometimes I was able to stop and say, "Enough. It's time to take a break and do something fun." I consciously sought to connect with and communicate with the deepest aspects of myself that I had repressed in childhood—what psychologists call the "dissociated" aspects of the personality. And I discovered that when a part of a person has been dissociated, that part doesn't have any memory of experiences beyond the age at which it was split off. The dissociated aspects of myself had not journeyed with me as I grew my confidence and self-esteem in adulthood. Those parts still felt that the only way to handle life with some degree of comfort and peace was to live through the presence of a cat.

So I talked to those parts of myself frequently, trying to help them understand that life could be good and they could experience love even though Emma was gone. Sometimes I felt those parts were listening, and sometimes I was even able to hear their thoughts and comfort them.

Animals teach us how to love unconditionally—pets fill in the gaps left in our hearts when our parents couldn't give us everything we needed. I wanted to learn how to love all of myself unconditionally in the same way, and not wait for someone else—feline or human—to give that to me. I even thought, *maybe I need to be as hedonistic as a cat.* After all, hedonism is really only an extreme attention paid to one's own needs and wants. But my childhood programming declared hedonism a sin. In fact, my programming even rejected the idea that I step forward and become the best self I could possibly be.

My life has been a constant battle with my childhood programming. Throughout the struggle, I've discovered aspects of myself that I never even knew existed.

In the midst of my work to reclaim the wonderful aspects of my self that I'd projected onto cats, I became aware of a much younger, deeper aspect of my psyche than I'd ever known before. It began with a flash of me sitting on the floor in diapers, staring at my pudgy legs and feet, with the carpeting beneath. When I finally had the opportunity to push everything else aside and get by myself so I could investigate this flash of memory, I was able to focus my consciousness into that part of myself that was sitting on the floor.

I noticed that in that memory, I wasn't looking at my mother, but I could feel her physical presence about ten feet in front of me, and her eternal presence all around me. And I noticed two more things: I didn't have a shirt on, and my diapers were too tight around my waist—it felt as if I was held there by a bar, unable to move forward. The feeling of a "bar" across my stomach, holding me in place, had recurred numerous times since my mother's death, every time I started to move forward or go for something I wanted.

I knew from past experience that exploring long-buried memories often yielded treasure in the form of freedom from old hurts and negative beliefs, so I gathered my strength for another round of clearing the past.

As I went deeper into the images and sensations of this "baby-self," I realized her mind felt almost empty. Compared to the adult "mind" I accept as mine—with its overflowing of tasks to do, ideas, hopes and dreams, and memories—my "mind" when I got inside that part of my head was nearly blank, lacking memories and knowledge, with almost no decision-making ability. There were very few experiences "embedded" in her mind, and her awareness was very free-floating and simple: "Me, her. My legs, floor," and there were no actual words, only images, sensations, and feelings. This is what makes me believe that I really did uncover and experience a heretofore buried part of myself.

As I sat with this infant memory, I allowed myself to feel her feelings. She was giving something up, staring at her little feet, sensing my mother somewhere in the room, and in her naive baby-knowing, she was realizing on a wordless level that she had to give up her sense of self and do what her mother wanted her to do in order to survive. She was deciding to make herself disappear so that mother could be number one, because she couldn't endure the hurt of struggling to get attention and being rejected anymore.

Though there weren't actual words in her mind, the feeling was "Her, not me," as she gave herself up in order to make life bearable. I believe she realized somehow that my mother would always be between me and the world, would always be unwilling to let me get "past" her and go out and live my own life.

For decades, I had always wondered why, throughout my life, I had just given in to my mother so quickly. I guess I learned early on that trying to get my own way only resulted in hurt and sadness. Time after time, I found myself at odds with my mother's desires. Even as an adult, no matter what I did or said, my mother continued beating on me verbally until I gave in. I never won in any situation, and I had never even wanted to fight. But she seemed to enjoy the battle. She had the stamina to continue a fight as long as necessary, and I had no stomach for it. And she was so needy that even as an adult, I could barely get going on a project before my mother interrupted and demanded my attention, as I wrote about in my memoir, *The Box of Daughter*.

I'm convinced now that when I was a baby, I made the only decision I could, and I am in awe that I made a choice at that young age that probably saved my sanity, and kept my sense of self intact, even if most of it was buried deep in my psyche for so many years. I'm sure that I would be a totally different person today if I'd continued to fight my mother and try to be first until she died.

For awhile, I made attempts to include this young part of my psyche in my day-to-day life, as if I had a new one-year-old baby in the house. I explained this and that, told her she could nap while I went to work, and tried to make room for doing some things that she wanted to do. I felt a sense of peace begin to radiate from her at times, though she still seemed to stretch out her awareness often to see if my mother was still there. This part had apparently still been dissociated when my mother passed away in 2005, and thought she was still around somewhere. Boy, I thought to myself, this little girl had been buried a LONG time!

I tried to encourage her on occasion to choose things that she wanted to do, and then reminded her that we were now the center of life for ourselves—that the mother energy was gone. I think she began to get the feeling that "mother" was no longer in the way.

Not too long after that, someone told me about a cat owner in their apartment building who had gone away for several weeks, and arranged for someone to take care of the cat—though the person only came in once or twice a week to feed the cat and dump the litter box. That very young part of my psyche hooked right in to the "poor kitty" and "how alone it must have felt"—and once I figured out that I was projecting my own feelings on this cat I didn't even know, I understood the desolation that long-buried part of my psyche had felt when she realized she had to give up all of her needs in order to try to make her mother happy so she didn't get hurt when she tried to get her way.

I tried more socializing, hoping that by getting more connected with others, I could heal that part of myself. But the problem wasn't a lack of people—I already had more than enough people in my life. The problem was the lack of a mirroring figure when I was small, a mirror in which to see my own needs and feelings, my own desires and enjoyments, my own sorrow and anger, my inner self reflected back to me so I could learn who I was becoming.

My mother had only seemed to see me as an extension of herself, and consequently, I *felt* like an extension—a half-person rather than a whole person. Even as an adult, I never felt like an adult, only a small-sized mirror of my mother. Lacking a mirror which showed me who I was and who I might become, I wasn't able to develop much of a sense of self, and even after almost thirty years of consistent work on self-discovery and self-esteem, my sense of self was still weak. It still wavered depending on circumstances, situations, other people's responses to me.

One night after some rich and satisfying socializing with good friends, I ended up in tears, missing Emma dreadfully. This confirmed my suspicion that it wasn't the company of other people I missed, it was a deep and steady connection with the cat who had been my best friend for seventeen years—the cat who whose presence had allowed my young self to give and receive the love I would have had from childhood if my mother had been able to open her heart to me.

Emma provided the steady, infinite love that the young aspect of my psyche needed, which went a long way toward healing my heart.

Most important, I think, Emma provided the mirror I'd never had—a being who was always happy to see me, who loved me more than anyone else, who was totally nonjudgmental; a being with a loving heart, a beautiful body, expressive eyes that told me she could see beyond all my problems and faults, and read the beauty of my soul. She taught me that another being could be reliable in its love for me, without asking that I give up myself and what I wanted. And she taught me that a relationship could progress on an even keel, that even when I was in the worst mood, or annoyed with her, or sad to my depths, she still loved me just the same, and would be there for me as long as she lived.

It seems odd to me that animals can provide the mothering that some of us so desperately missed in childhood, when humans are supposed to be smarter than animals. But I'm not sure that's so.

Chapter 7: The Littlest One

One of the hardest things to give up after Emma's passing was knowing that I was the most important person in her life. Growing up with two narcissistic parents, I had never known the joy of being the most important person to someone else.

I'd always had to make other people more important than I was. Even as an adult, I continually put other people first—and though this can be an admirable quality when not taken to extremes, it also caused me to feel small and insignificant, and ignore my own needs at the expense of my mental and physical health.

I wanted this "baby self" I'd discovered to feel just as important as everyone else, because I imagined that if I could get her to understand her own significance and power, my self-esteem would grow, and in learning to meet my own needs and live life in a way that worked best for me, I could achieve even more. I knew that loving Emma in all her natural, wild, uninhibited freedom had probably been my way of loving that part of myself—the part that longed to be totally free to be whoever I wanted to be—and I thought that "feeding" this part of myself was a step on the path to finding that freedom. I tried to make it clear that now *she* could be number one, and she didn't have to make parts of herself disappear anymore.

I tried to help her understand that when she made herself "disappear" in order to put my mother first, she might have made herself disappear into cats so she could feel at least a little loved by my mother, who was completely enamored of cats. Though it seems silly as I write about it, the experience was a very profound one. I also figured that by "disappearing myself" at an early age, I probably held myself back from success, from fulfilling my potential throughout my life, and I wanted to change that.

I knew that since this early part of my psyche had been "split off"—relegated to hiding deep within my memories in order to keep me safe—she had no knowledge of my life past the age of two. I could tell she still worried that my mother would show up out of the blue, which meant that she hadn't been part of my awareness when my mother passed away. This little self-fragment wasn't aware of what I'd learned about boundaries, what I'd accomplished, how I'd learned to protect myself, and how safe I felt with most of the people in my life. She was virtually stuck in the time when she had made that decision.

I discovered one day in meditation that though it didn't really help to *tell* her how my life was very different now—because she had very few language skills—it did help to *show* her in mind-pictures, and share the feeling of being safe, of being more whole, with her. In the meditation, I went back to the age at which I'd made that early decision, consciously connected with that part of my psyche, and took her through a visualization of all the years of my life from the time she had cut herself off up to the present, so that she could experience, at least for a few moments, all of what I have experienced.

In my mind, this was the only way to bring a dissociated aspect of myself "up to speed" in my life so that she could learn that it's okay to trust, that good things can happen, and that love can be found anywhere and everywhere—that she doesn't have to have a cat around in order to experience love.

My inner child had a terrible fear of abandonment because my parents had emotionally abandoned me at an early age, and there was likely nothing I could do to change that, no matter how hard I tried. But during the seventeen years I'd had Emma, she had never abandoned me. Knowing Emma would always be there, as long as she was alive, was very healing. So I tried to offer that same feeling to this inner-child aspect of myself.

When I finally began to acknowledge and heal my early feelings of abandonment, I understood the intensely sad feelings of the small child I was when she realized that her parents would never give her what she needed, and I re-experienced the horror of having no one else to turn to for years at a time. I think this must be part of what philosophers call "existential angst"—the feeling that we truly are alone in life, and though others may love us and lend helping hands, we are still alone with ourselves in the midst of our life experiences.

Focusing on taking care of Emma had allowed me to continue to hide from myself the profound sadness I'd felt as a child at the absence of a loving bond with my parents—or even a basic sense of being respected by them. As I connected more often with this dissociated aspect of myself, the wound at the core of my deepest self opened up and spewed out its despair, anger, frustration, and shame at not ever having felt loved by my mother.

In my grieving, I came face to face with the feelings of how much my parents had hurt me with their emotional abuse. Over and over, throughout the first fifty years of my life, they had criticized me, shamed me, insulted me, and rejected the deepest, most vulnerable aspects of my inner self.

I knew I could probably assuage those emotions by quickly running out to get another pet—but I also knew that I would never heal if I continued to seek out substitutes and allow myself to let that pain go into hiding again, become part of my unconscious "shadow," and wreak more havoc in my life.

I don't imagine my parents were aware of how their criticism and rejection wounded me, but that didn't make it any less difficult to face. Through her unconditional love, Emma had taught me what it was like to feel appreciated, respected, nourished, and cared for—day in and day out—and it became very clear to me how much of a void was inside of me, a void I'd lived with for my entire life.

Somehow I knew that if I kept relying on pets to meet my need to be loved, I would never be able to open my heart enough to find love with other human beings, and I would never learn how to love myself. So I decided that I would wait to get another pet until I had unraveled more of the unhealthy messages I received about love from childhood.

The feeling of "blank awareness" I had experienced in the meditation with the younger aspect of myself intrigued me—it seemed so much more open to possibility, infinity, and the Universe than my usual monkey mind, so, motivated by this discovery, I decided to explore my relationship with myself and the Universe, and to try to heal this deeply wounded part of me before I got another cat. I wanted to uncover the parts of myself that I had "submerged" into my relationship with cats, and bring them into full expression in my life rather than just experiencing them vicariously.

I tried to find a part of myself that could believe that I was perfect just as I am, the same way I saw Emma. Animals are just who they are, with no excuses, no judgment, no guilt. I wanted to learn to feel that way about myself.

As I sank into the memories of my bond with Emma—how deep and sweet and almost painful-in-its-strength that love was—the veil that had covered the sorrow I felt as a child started to lift. I began to process the decades-old grief I carried, along with the subliminal distress that had always pervaded my life because I hadn't known what was missing in childhood or how to get it. I only knew that the love I felt for Emma and that I knew she felt for me was similar to what should have existed with my parents.

And as tears filled my eyes, I could actually sense my infant self in that moment—I felt its total confusion and heartbreak at not receiving what it wanted and needed. In the midst of this new experience of grieving for that heartbroken part of myself came an early half-memory of my mother giving me a toy, and then when I'd gotten interested in it, taking it back. In this way, my attention became riveted on her and I lost track of my own desires. I realized I'd developed an early belief that I couldn't get what I wanted, and I couldn't ever keep anything I received.

Since my mother loved to be the center of attention, no doubt she thought it was a fun game, but from that game I learned that energy and things could be taken from me at any time, and I would receive very little. Sadly, that unconscious expectation has informed most of my life experience—thus my fervent desire to heal as much as I could, and change my life for the better.

Early memories came to me almost in a half-light, with no words attached, because they occurred before I knew how to use words. But the sensations and feelings were very clear.

The terrible bone-deep feeling that the infant-me had simply given up ever getting anything she wanted and had lain unmoving, curled up in a ball deep within my psyche for 50 years, began to permeate my sadness. Trying to provide a corrective experience, I experimented with pointing out things around my apartment, as if I was letting my infant self choose what she wanted, and reassuring her, "No one will ever take that away— you can have it for always." I repeated this over a period of a few days, and I sensed that she began to uncurl a bit, saying what she wanted, expressing opinions and likes and dislikes, just the way a child would if she began to feel safe, began to feel she was loved.

I wanted more than anything for that part of myself to feel taken care of and loved, the way I took care of Emma and loved her. In my caring for Emma, this small part of me was able to experience, at least vicariously, what it was like to have someone love her unconditionally. As I worked with her energy, I found myself saying to the Universe, "I just want to be loved and cared for the way I loved and cared for Emma." This little "infant" part of my psyche, which had been "hiding" in Emma, projecting herself on cats because somehow she figured out that they were the only ones in our family who got love, respect, and consideration, was finally getting a chance to speak her deepest needs and desires.

This connection with more primal aspects of myself was what I had been hoping would happen if I focused on finding a deeper connection with myself instead of getting another cat right away. I wish the process of growing beyond old habitual patterns and integrating dissociated aspects of myself hadn't been so painful. But that's part of the healing process: being willing to experience the pain and sadness, letting it overcome us so that we can fully express it, and then finally releasing it so we can heal and move forward.

Throughout the process of grieving deeply for Emma, I realized that in spite of the abuse I'd experienced from my parents, I still managed to retain a great capacity for love. I wondered how one small kitty could inspire an infinite outpouring of love from my heart and soul. Where had that capacity to love come from? How did I learn it? Why wasn't it destroyed? I desperately wanted to find a way to express that love to the world, to the Universe, to myself, and to find it reflected by the world, the Universe, and myself. How and where could I express that depth of love again? How and where could I experience it coming back to me?

For most of my life, I've felt disconnected from the world—as if I was never completely planted in earthly life. Part of this, I'm sure, was my extreme sensitivity to all things energetic and emotional—the "life" under the surface of life—and hypervigilance developed in childhood to keep myself from being hurt. I truly wanted to find a way to "fit in" to the world, to feel like I belonged here, to develop a loving relationship with the Universe and other human beings.

I recognized that I needed to extend the love I felt for Emma to all of creation—good or bad, happy or sad—to flowers and skunks and trees and rats, just because all are expressions of the Creator's energy. I think that the more difficult something is to love, the more of a challenge it is. And perhaps, sometimes the more difficult it is to love, the more it *needs* love.

I came to realize that because I'd missed out on the experience of love, I'd never developed a connection to the Universe that would allow it to express its love for me. For I do believe that Life and the Universe want to love and support us, just as life force energy supports the plants and animals on the earth. It didn't seem right to limit my lovingness to my relationships with cats and a few people here and there. I began to reach out to the love around me—sending love to the birds at the birdfeeder, to the chipmunks as they scrabbled for their meals beneath it.

There was one bird in particular, very small and possibly new to the world, who would sit on one side of the feeder for hours at a time, just looking around at everything. I began to think of this bird as my friend, sending love to it as I watched it through the sliding glass door. Sometimes it would sit facing the door, as if it felt something, or was waiting for me to come out and show myself.

One day I did. I slid the door open as quietly as I could, and just stood there for a moment. The bird kept staring at me. Slowly lifting my foot and gently emerging onto the patio, I kept sending love in the bird's direction. The feeder swayed a bit as if the bird was trembling, but it held its ground. After a few moments, I eased back inside. After that, as long as I moved slowly and kept a gentle focus on the bird, it would stay while I came out to stand on the patio.

Such courage!—to stand its ground when a being 100 times bigger approached. Maybe love makes that kind of courage possible.

I persisted in the challenging work of expressing my feelings in order to heal one of the deepest wounds a person can have—a lack of mothering—and began to seek out other ways to meet my needs to be loved. I decided that I wanted to face the world the way Emma had: offering love whenever I could, expressing myself to the fullest, and clearly asking for what I needed, expecting that, with patience, my needs would be met.

Deep down, I thought that maybe when you stop looking for love in just one place, you might discover that it's everywhere.

Chapter 8: No Regrets

I've always believed that we continue somewhere, somehow after we leave our physical form on this earth. In the months after Emma's death, I felt that her spirit was often around, and when I missed her, I tried to tune into her spirit for comfort. I admitted to myself and to her spirit that for the last six months of her life, though I had absolutely wanted her to make the final decision about when she wanted to go, there was a part of me that had been ready to be alone, that was ready to let go of all responsibility for other living things.

In essence, there was a part of me that was almost eagerly waiting for her to show me a sign that she wanted to leave. After caring for my elderly parents for so many years, I was tired of feeling that others, whether they were cats or people, were demanding my attention when I wanted to give it to myself.

Looking back, I know there were times when I treated Emma with less than total respect and love, especially in the last year of her life when life was particularly hard for me in terms of my business and work. Sometimes when I was working in my office, she would sneak up behind me and suddenly meow, and more often than not in the last year of her life, I would say, "Just a minute" in the same tone of voice my mother had used with me, then proceed to work for another five minutes while she sat there and waited. Sometimes I felt that her needs were an interruption; instead of responding with love, I responded with annoyance.

For months after she was gone, I was filled with regret—for
all the times I'd complained when she simply asked for food,
for all the times I'd felt she was a burden as much as a friend.
Still recovering from the dysfunctional relationship with my
parents, having another creature need me was frustrating at
times because it reminded me of how needy my parents had been.

And it wasn't that Emma was overly needy—in fact, she
generally kept to herself most of the time, though she was almost
always open to my affection, when I took the time to be with her.
Life was a struggle at that point—as a single householder and a
creative person, it was difficult to make ends meet when the
economy sank, and though I spent time with Emma every day, I
never felt it was enough. Frustration and guilt bubbled up on a
regular basis.

One morning she woke me up early, as she sometimes did.
I'd been working too hard, pushing myself, with too many tasks
and people demanding too much of me. I was so tired and
frustrated, and without thinking, I just yelled at her to leave me
alone, something I'd never done before, and will never do again
with a pet. The surprise and confusion on her face almost made
me cry. I apologized immediately, and I regret that moment of
weakness to this day. I wonder now if it brought back painful
memories for her of the time she lived across the hall from me.
And I wonder how animals experience memory, and emotion, as
compared to the ways in which humans do.

But through it all, she loved me constantly. She was always
willing to give me love, and that aspect of our relationship was

deeply healing for me. Love from my mother and father had been totally conditional, dependent on my being who they wanted me to be, on my always being there for them emotionally. Until Emma, I had never known the feeling of being loved no matter who I was, how I felt, or what I did. Her constant love was an incredible gift for me.

Regrets...what do we do with them after the fact? They weigh us down and make us feel guilty—yet animals are unconditionally forgiving, and on some level, I think they understand some of the difficulties we humans encounter, and they don't seem to judge us.

I felt so ashamed that I'd been so ready to let Emma go, and I imagined that she might have sensed my ambivalence in the last months of her life. One day I decided to apologize to her spirit and ask for forgiveness, and I immediately felt as if she lifted her face to mine and touched my nose, which in our relationship seemed to be the way she expressed her greatest love for me. I heard the words, "No regrets" in my mind, and I felt a deep and forgiving sense of love behind them, wherever they came from.

Tears ran down my cheeks as I sensed her communicating that she had understood my feelings, and that she forgave me in every way. I hope that someday I'll be able to say the same thing, and mean it from the bottom of my heart, when I think of my parents. And myself.

In contrast, when I was small and made mistakes, I would always apologize profusely to my mother, desperately wanting her to love me even after I had disappointed her. "I'm sorry," I would say, with all the love I had pouring out of my heart.

Every time, my mother responded, "I'm sorry, too" in a disgruntled tone of voice—and 'til the day she died, I felt that she never forgave me for all the ways I didn't measure up to what she wanted. I know now that it wasn't that I didn't do everything I possibly could to get her love; rather, she was unable or unwilling to express her love and satisfaction with my efforts. Emma's gift of compassion in my grieving washed those years of sadness away as I felt her total forgiveness.

I truly believe that our animal companions do not hold grudges, that they do not judge their owners in any way. I believe that their love for us far outweighs any mistakes that we, as loving owners, might commit. I know it's different when an animal is abused, but this is why I love animals so much: they are as totally giving as most people naturally are when they're children.

In many cases, that natural human capacity for love and generosity of spirit that's often so obvious in young children gets beaten down by the criticism and judgment of those who take care of us, or by the simple fact that we have to learn to sublimate so many of our emotions and needs in order to interact in a "civilized" way with others around us.

Yes, pets are "domesticated"—which in my mind means they've learned how to get along with people without losing their natural sense of self. But people get "civilized"—twisted into shapes and personalities that have to fit into the structure of our dysfunctional society, often without retaining much of that natural sense of self.

I hope one day people have as much compassion for each other as I think animals have for their owners. And I believe that one of the reasons we can love our animal companions so deeply is that they reflect back to us our own beauty, wisdom, generosity, lack of pretense, spontaneity, and infinite capacity for love.

I continued my quest to broaden my connection with the Universe and my deeper self in the hope that I wouldn't be so dependent on my love of pets. I knew that if I continued to "depend" on pets as my only loving bond, I would continue to be devastated every time one of my pets died. So I persisted, even though my life felt very empty without a cat.

The next natural step was to find out how to accept the same kind of constant love that Emma had given me from the Universe, and from myself—a big hurdle for me. Throughout my life, I'd been made to feel that I had to be a certain way or do certain things in order to be loved, and I needed to learn that I am lovable no matter who I am or what I do. Emma totally changed that vibration for me.

I wonder if other pet owners might feel that the only way their true selves can be loved is through their relationships with animals.

Though I regretted the pattern I had fallen into of being irritated with Emma's needs, of wanting to ignore her needs because I wasn't getting my own needs met in other ways, the experience was a great lesson for me. I learned that in wanting to ignore her needs, I was also ignoring my own needs for affection, love, and enjoyment—a habit I learned completely and thoroughly in childhood.

And that brought me to a realization of how much I'd been abusing myself, exactly the way my parents did: not allowing time for myself, not allowing myself to have my needs be met, not allowing myself to succeed, not allowing myself to follow my inner guidance—all of these are ways that my parents abused me, and I saw that I had been doing the same things to myself.

I began pondering how I might rediscover self-care without always depending on pets for it.

Since one of the things I'd enjoyed about taking care of Emma was a feeling of allowing myself time for gentleness and love and affection and connection on a deep level, I resolved to try to give myself regular times of connection and affection. Having a relationship with a local bird was one way to do that. I love being out in nature, and I made an effort to give myself more time for that. I also made sure to take time for things I enjoy— reading novels, working on jigsaw puzzles, and creating art.

I also made attempts to "open more conversations" with younger aspects of myself: the child part of my psyche who had been neglected, as well as a part of myself that felt a little older— maybe 10—and had given all of her attention to her very introverted dad at the expense of her own needs. I tried to include those parts of me in decisions now and then, asked about what they wanted to do, and tried to provide it—hoping to create a "corrective experience" that would heal some of the years of rejection.

What I missed most was Emma's sweetness—she was such a lovely, sweet, beautiful soul—and I realized over time that that same quality is actually within me as well, and she was just reflecting who I am on every level. But that tender aspect of myself had been so hurt, so damaged in childhood, that the only way it could express itself was through a bond with cats. Relationships with other people didn't usually feel safe to me, because of my childhood experiences. Expressing that "sweetness" with people made me feel way too vulnerable.

I was afraid that if I allowed myself to feel and express that vulnerability, I could be terribly hurt and frightened again as I'd been when I was young. It didn't feel safe to allow myself to feel or express tenderness in relation to other people, so I saw it in Emma instead. In my quest to protect her in every way I could, I was protecting that aspect of myself. But I wanted to find that sweetness elsewhere in my life—it's such a beautiful emotion, and adds joy and tenderness to our lives.

I think we are all so heavily armored against our vulnerability and deep feelings that we miss infinite opportunities for joy, wonder, and love in our lives. Or we confine those deeper aspects of ourselves to a very small portion of our connection with others. This is the aspect of living in society that saddens me the most. Life could be much different.

I have been able to express my vulnerability and sweetness with a few people in my life, and it brings me great joy. But it's always like just a little peek of sun on a cloudy day. Intimacy is a scary thing, and I admire people who do it well and feel good about it.

In my quest to discover more of myself, I thought about all of the things I missed about Emma which I knew were most likely aspects of myself that had never been integrated: her sweetness; her wildness when she was hunting; her delicacy and beauty; the perfection of her soul and her physical self; her constancy and love; her willingness to keep asking when she wanted something without guilt (I imagine)—and her trust that she would eventually get it; her whimsicality; her love of comfort and pleasure; even her loving attention to herself when she washed and groomed. I wanted to use Emma as a sort of "role model," and learn to accept all those qualities as aspects of myself and integrate them into my image of who I am.

With no other understanding of life, myself, or other people as a child, the way I saw myself was through my parents' eyes, because my self-image developed based on the way they treated me. And as a child, when I saw myself from their point of view, I wasn't supposed to be lovable. I wasn't supposed to be smart, or affectionate, or beautiful, or wild, or free, or behaving naturally in the moment as my soul moved me. I was only supposed to be a dutiful daughter, a mirror for their needs—an emotional support, giving whatever they needed and being whoever they needed me to be in the moment. Everything that was "me" was stripped away and became identified with cats.

Even now, I find it hard to believe that for fifty years, I lived the life of a dutiful-daughter-robot, while my soul continued to make its home within each cat I had come to love.

When my parents were alive, I often seemed to have trouble coping with day-to-day living in the world, and as I look back, I see that it's partly because I only learned to function within the world as a false self—as the daughter/person my parents wanted me to be—so I wasn't able to use my natural strengths and intelligence the way most people do; and partly because I was so identified with the "inner life of cats" that I had trouble identifying with the world of humans. And of course, my parents' constant criticism and neediness kept me from reaching deep within myself and connecting with my strength and competence.

My "cat role-model" showed me how to be unconditionally loving, and gave me the desire to live with complete self-integrity and the freedom to express myself and love myself just as I am. The "cat role-model" offered me a view of life in which the self could express itself totally, with fierceness at times and absolute tenderness at times, totally nonjudgmental of others, and in touch with all of life.

There are some groups of humans who operate in a similar way, but so much of the world seems more to reflect my parents' way of being: rigidity, selfishness, and chaos, living within a very narrow framework that doesn't allow much room for the soul. Living within the concepts of this soulful role-model makes me a round peg in a square hole in our society. And it seems there's no way to change that. How does one reconcile the feeling that one's truest sense of self is in a state of uncomfortable disharmony with today's society?

One morning I woke up from a dream in which I went to rescue Emma from a government office. She was in a large cage, feeling frustrated and sad beyond belief because she'd given up hope that I would ever come and rescue her. She was so relieved that I had come—and I realized that in the dream Emma represented my self, feeling boxed in by my parents for 50 years, waiting endlessly and sadly for me to come and rescue myself.

As the dream reverberated within me for the next few days, I became more determined to stop denying the beautiful part of myself that reflects cats—the part that wants to be completely free to express itself. I wanted to change my life so that all the parts of me could be free. But I didn't know how.

Emma had been my primary connection to the beauty and glory of the Universe, when everything else around me was painful and unwelcoming. One of the things I most appreciated about Emma was that she was such a glorious and free expression of Infinite Intelligence. I wanted to find a way to expand my connection to the beauty and glory of the Universe into my whole world, to permeate my entire life with it so that I could experience in myriad, bountiful ways that one small, joyful part of my life that Emma had represented.

Emma truly connected me with my beingness—that state of being totally who I am and totally in the moment that everything in nature achieves all the time, but that humans fall out of repeatedly in the quest to do more and be more. I lost my connection with my beingness when I lost Emma.

Emma had always encouraged my soul to come forward—to rest in the midst of work, to stop and enjoy her beauty, to indulge in love and affection, reminding me that the soul needs space to expand and appreciate, to rest and recharge itself. Without Emma, I was just a "human doing." I didn't know how to just "be" without a cat in my life to remind me.

After Emma was gone, I struggled to learn how to stop doing and just "be." One dark, rainy night when I went for a late walk, I finally understood why Emma loved to be out in the night so much. My soul reached out to the heavens, even though they were filled with clouds and haze, and I could almost feel the trees sunk into their earthly beds, patiently waiting for the return of the sun while they rested from the reaching they did during the day. The drizzle caressed my skin gently, as if a thousand tiny pats of love from the Universe were falling on me. I was truly completely immersed in "being."

In the quiet of the night, in the dark and open space, I felt bigger. I felt real. I felt that my wild, natural self was connected to everything—connected in a way that I've never been able to feel in the midst of people. Why do we all talk so much when there is so much to be felt and experienced? When there is so much to open up to? I'm not a big talker; in fact, I have always been the person that people talk and talk and talk at. But I think talking is often a defense against opening up to a deep and true connection with the world. For me, even a good conversation rarely compares to the communion I felt with Emma, and which I often feel with nature. Maybe that's just the way I'm made, or maybe it's a result of my experience with people in childhood.

On that night, I discovered a wild, free, natural part of myself, submerged since childhood, which I'd kept alive by living it vicariously through the cats in my life. I needed to find a safe way to express my wilder, primordial side so it didn't completely go into hiding again. That wildness and fierceness is part of my strength, so I didn't want to lose it or suppress it again. I know that the more we repress our wilder or "shadow" urges, the stronger they become—and eventually they burst out, often wreaking havoc in our lives, and sometimes in the lives of others.

The only way I'd ever found to express my wilder side was dancing—turning on music and just moving however my body wanted to move. But I wanted more. I wanted to live through that wild and natural part of myself all the time, and see how my entire life might change. I wondered if it was even possible to live that way in the midst of a generally dysfunctional society.

How do cats manage to live with humans, I wonder, and so easily forgive and forget our many foibles?

I often felt Emma's presence. Sometimes when I wasn't even thinking about her, she would suddenly come to mind when I was near her favorite sleeping spot, almost as if I'd heard her meow. I would stop for a moment and appreciate her presence, and I always felt love flowing back.

Sometimes the connection with her was so strong that I almost felt as if she was about to "pop" into physical existence. I was totally surprised and overwhelmed on Christmas morning when I logged onto Facebook and saw her photo shining out at me over the caption "See Your Year." I had posted it many months before in February as a memorial. I thought to myself, "Out of all the photos I posted this year, what are the chances that this one photo would come up to lead the reminders of the past year?" Totally awesome. It was as if Emma herself had shown up to wish me a Merry Christmas.

Life is very strange at times, but I think that's exactly how it's supposed to be—that we're supposed to get caught up in the mystery of it all, the wonder and awe at the strange ways in which the Universe works. I loved the idea that Emma was visiting for Christmas, and marveled once again at the infinite possibilities of Life and the Universe. I felt that the Universe was holding out a special gift for me in that moment, almost as if it was expressing its love for me through a picture of Emma. In that moment, in the midst of deep emotion, I reached out to the Universe, expressing my wish to experience the feeling that I'm loved by whatever power, intelligence, and spirit is out there, and to know that I can love myself the way I loved Emma, and that the Universe can be there for me always, the way Emma was.

When I think about how much our animal friends trust us to take care of them, I realize that I'd like to believe that the Universe takes care of us in the same way. When we don't always provide what our animal friends need five seconds after they ask,

I don't think they have the same doubts that plague the human mind, like "What if she doesn't bring food?" "What if she decides not to this time?"

I imagine Emma knew I would always bring food when she was hungry. I never knew whether or not my parents would give me what I asked for, so I'm hardwired for doubt. I wanted to integrate into my psyche the assurance that our needs are always provided for—maybe not at exactly the moment we ask, but that the Universe does indeed love and support us. I needed to learn how to have faith.

Chapter 9: The Fuzzy Face of God

For decades, I had reached out to try and develop a loving relationship with a higher power. I couldn't quite call it God, because that brought up memories of the vengeful and angry God of my childhood, which was represented in my father when he beat my brother in a fit of holy rage. The Disciples of Christ Church, where we were members, taught submission, guilt, and fear, and I wanted to overcome its religious indoctrination and find a personal connection with the Universe, in a form that felt right to me.

I tried thinking of a higher power as "infinite intelligence," and that worked a little better. I tried thinking of it as female—a mother-goddess—but that didn't feel right to me either, possibly because of the difficult relationship I had with my mother. I finally settled on "All That Is" until I could come up with a better name or image.

I'd been brought up to believe that God was judgmental, strict, and unloving, punishing even the smallest offense, and rarely showing mercy. I never could understand how a God like that could be merciful, too, except that it meant he might let you off the hook for awhile if you did enough good things for others. The church community's perspective on doing good was that if you gave enough, you might have enough points to get into heaven by the time you died. But nobody ever explained how the point system worked—so I just turned into the Good Little Girl, always giving, never demanding, in the hope of avoiding hell.

On an intuitive level, I didn't believe that that kind of God could have created such a beautiful universe, spilling out gorgeous sunsets, astonishing animals, stunning plants and flowers, and above all, love. But I did sense some kind of intelligence under the surface of the world that makes acorns grow into oak trees instead of ears of corn, and bulbs become flowers instead of animals.

Over the years, I'd connected on a sensation/awareness level with *something*—I could feel a presence around me, and deep down I knew something had brought me into this life for a purpose; but not having known what parental love felt like as a child, I could not perceive love coming from the Universe, even though I believed it was essentially benevolent. If "it" didn't want us here, I'm sure we would have been gone by now.

I wrestled with the conflict between what I felt and believed as an adult, and the beliefs I'd developed in childhood that everything around me had its own agenda, and that unless I played by its rules and did everything right, I would be hurt and abandoned.

One day, missing Emma, I thought about her spirit floating and playing somewhere "out there" in the Universe, or at least in some dimension that I can't perceive with my five senses, and I sent a feeling of love to her, smiling and blinking my eyes the way we used to do when we were together. I realized that I was expanding my feeling of "sending love" from sending it to a small creature in a physical body to sending it out into the Universe to land wherever it might. And I suddenly felt love *coming back to me*—I didn't know whether it was from Emma's spirit or the Universe as a whole, but in that moment I realized that there is love all around us, all the time—and that whatever intelligence is intrinsic to or scattered throughout this physical world wants us to be here, wants to nourish us, and is open to communication on an intuitive or sensation level.

This was what I had been looking for all the time—a feeling of connectedness, of being joined with All That Is on a heart level. I had found love with Emma, and she'd helped me learn how to love myself—and now she was teaching me how to reach out to the universe with love, and allow its love to return.

Emma had been a kind of "interface" between All That Is and me—she offered a way for me to access the light, love, beauty, simplicity, and gentleness of the Universe. She fed my soul and taught me to nourish my spirituality.

I had always seen Emma as a part of myself, and I often felt as if I was relating to myself as much as to her when we were together. But without her presence, I was having difficulty allowing and expressing all the wonderful qualities that I ascribed to cats. My childhood programming—the "shoulds" and "oughts"—kept bumping up against my yearning to grow and explore and become all that I wanted to be. It was as if I needed cats to "interface" with both my innermost self and the Universe.

I made a conscious effort to begin sending love to myself—when I caught my own eye in the mirror, when I lay in bed in the morning between alarm-clock rings, and when I was not feeling up to par. I imagined smiling down at all of my organs at times; I crossed my arms and hugged myself now and then, as if I were hugging Emma. I also encouraged myself to spend more time in nature, to take more moments to appreciate the beauty of the Universe, to dance with abandon in order to express the wild, fierce instincts that I think are, deep down, still a part of human life.

I felt very selfish and self-centered and self-focused, which totally opposed my programming. I was "supposed" to be giving, unselfish, and totally focused on the needs of others. But living by that programming was exactly what had caused me to lose myself in the first place. So I persisted in my quest, and told the old voices to shut up whenever they bothered me.

One morning, after mourning my loss yet again, I decided to meditate. I asked for healing and compassion, and I felt a cloud of caring enveloping me. As I leaned into this energy of compassion, I suddenly felt what seemed to be other souls or soul-energies gathering around me for an energetic "group hug." As I leaned further into that support and asked for my pain to be taken away, I felt more and more of these energies—many individuals, but all connected—gathering around me until there seemed to be hundreds, then thousands, surrounding me, offering support, each taking a little bit of the pain so that none were overwhelmed. It was as if the pain was spread out over thousands so there was no need for one soul—myself—to bear it all.

I stayed in this meditation for about ten minutes, feeling the pain drain away, and breathing in the support and love coming my way. As someone who has never been very comfortable in large groups of people, it amazed me that I felt completely at ease surrounded by all of these energies, and I expressed my gratitude and love. I felt a deep well of love bloom inside of me that wanted to be expressed—the same bottomless flow that I had given and received with Emma. At that moment, I knew that I would be able to find the same kind of love I'd had with Emma out in the world—maybe not all at once, maybe not all in one place—but I would find it eventually.

The more I searched, the more experiences of connection came to me.

I love the idea of God as the "quantum field" that surrounds us—the infinite inherent intelligence of the cosmic soup of molecules, atoms, and quarks that make up the universe we live in. I know that *something* is out there, and thinking of God as the quantum field removes all the old fear of judgment that's burned into my brain.

One night, taking a bath and immersing myself in the idea of the quantum field, I suddenly heard a voice saying, "I invite you to become me." I don't know whether it came from my thoughts, or from the Universe, but all of a sudden I felt merged with everything—there was no sense of separateness between me and the world, between me and the trees, between me and animals, between me and other people. I felt "bonded" to and with the

Universe the same way I had felt bonded with Emma, almost as if we were twin aspects of the same soul.

Even with occasional experiences like this, I still couldn't seem to find a deep, consistent connection with the Universe. As soon as I focused on the practicalities of life, it disappeared, and life became empty again. And I wanted that connection as badly as I had wanted my mother's love when I was small.

I woke up in tears one morning not long after that, missing Emma, wondering what the heck I was supposed to do with all the love that still wanted to pour out of me into taking care of the beautiful, wild, fierce, gentle, loving cat that had been an integral part of my life for so many years. In my mind, I tried to refocus that love to my inner child, offering her the comfort and affection and encouragement that she'd never received from her parents.

And suddenly, I felt as if the relationship was reversed: instead of *my* being the one that "took care of" and cared for a small, sweet, vulnerable other, the Universe was caring for the small, sweet, vulnerable self that was me—as if I was the pet, and the Universe was the caretaker.

The feeling of being taken care of was foreign to me. I began to let go of my habit of always being the caretaker, and let myself learn what it feels like to be taken care of. And I suddenly saw that it's *people* that hurt us, not the Universe. The Universe only wants the best for us. And people will sometimes hurt us, intentionally or not, but the Universe will always support us.

In that moment, I just let go of the struggle to take care of myself, and began to allow the Universe to take care of me. To me, this meant that I could finally express the beauty, vulnerability, and wild fierceness and playfulness of my soul, and place the cares of my life into the Universe's hands. I could surrender and allow the Universe to encourage and support me, to love and care for me, to take care of me in every way.

It took me awhile to feel "worthy" of being taken care of by the Universe, because of my childhood programming that I could never be good enough. Looking back, I think this was the point at which I gave up my view of the Universe as a reflection of my parents and the judgmental God of my childhood. In any case, the world around me seemed to change, to soften, almost to smile, in the following weeks.

I believe in offering oneself as a vessel for the creative spirit—whether one is a writer, artist, musician, or anything else, even if it doesn't pertain to the arts—and I've come to believe that we're supposed to allow ourselves to be taken care of in return. After all, we're expressing the deepest longings and possibilities that the Universe has to offer.

I had truly enjoyed being adored by Emma—being greeted with love and enthusiasm, getting head butts, hearing the purr that came only for me, even knowing that although she hid when other people were nearby, she loved being with me. I want to believe that the Universe adores us in the same way that our pets do—that it adores not only our humanness, but our determination to survive, our sometimes feeble attempts to keep moving forward and to express the beauty and glory of All That

Is. I think it adores us as a perfect mother would adore her child. And I asked myself, how could I connect to that adoration from the Universe, instead of assuming it was gone because Emma was dead?

My inner child craved so much tenderness and affection, like someone who'd been starved for decades. It was becoming more clear that I had cared for this small part of me through caring for Emma—and that my relationship with Emma was in a lot of ways a substitute for a loving, caring relationship with myself. In order to develop that relationship with myself, I needed to discover inside myself all of the wonderful qualities I'd projected on cats because I had believed I didn't have them. I had to see those qualities "outside of myself" and experience them in a deeply bonded relationship before I could fully accept and appreciate them in myself.

I needed to allow the "good and beautiful" side of myself to become my new self-image, and release the defective, imperfect self-image I'd identified with in childhood. I needed to learn to love myself as much for those qualities as I had always loved Emma.

A few weeks later, I went out one morning to clear the snow off my car. As I brushed away the snow from the windshield, I saw a large, clear, heart-shaped patch of ice underneath, smack in the middle of the driver's-side section of the windshield—an awe-inspiring symbol of the love I had sent out to the Universe coming back to me.

I read once that everything in the world loves us: that flowers, trees, and rocks can love us if we let them. But the heart on my windshield was more than that: to me, it was a symbol of Life itself choosing to demonstrate its love for me.

Chapter 10: Pets of the Universe

That night, I started praying, asking the Universe to help me find the love and joy I'd found with Emma. I consciously focused on reaching out, trying to create the same bond with the cosmos that I'd had with Emma. Words welled up from within, and I let them flow, as I felt my inner child expressing her innermost needs to the cosmos in a way that she never could with my parents.

"Please always always love me the way Emma did."

Tears began to run down my face as I remembered the feeling of never being loved by my parents, simmering under and through the feeling of being loved that I'd finally found with Emma, like the dark, mucky bottom of a pond that shines with sparkles from the sun on top.

"Please always always be there for me the way she was."

"Please always always let me know that I'm good enough just as I am, the way she did."

My inner child began to let go of years of never feeling good enough.

"Please always always make me feel better the way she did."

"Please always always greet me happily when you see me."

In my mind's eye, I saw Emma bounding down from the bed, happily purring as she rubbed against my leg.

"Please always always bring joy to my life like she did."

"Please always always comfort me the way Emma did."

I thought of all the years I'd wanted comfort from my parents, and finally found it with Emma.

"Please always always let me feel like I belong, the way she helped me belong."

"Please always always be my best reflection, like she was."

In that moment, I understood deep within the core of my being that I had always felt as if the Universe itself reflected my parents—judgmental, unforgiving, withholding, indifferent to my needs, and disappointed in me—and that I'd always responded to it as if it was my mother or father, trying to please it so it wouldn't hurt me. I wanted to develop a belief that the cosmos, whatever Intelligence was out there, was more like Emma: loving, dependable, generous, and comforting. I wanted to recreate the world around me in the image of Emma, and dissolve the old belief that the Intelligence at the center of the Universe saw me as my parents saw me, and treated me as my parents had treated me.

I wanted to unravel and banish 50 years' worth of negative programming so that my real self could shine out into my life and walk with joy and confidence into my future.

I thought about the way in which Emma might have seen me as her friend and caretaker, and oddly, suddenly wondered what it would be like to be the Universe's "pet." For some even stranger reason, the 23rd Psalm came into my head, and I started visualizing what the human-animal bond might be like from a pet's perspective.

My person is my shepherd, I shall not want.
She petteth my head and admireth my beauty,
She giveth me food and water when I am hungry,
She restoreth my soul.
She helpeth me understand that humans are on the side of
*   animals.*

Yea, though I go out at night to hunt,
I know that she will be waiting when I return home,
Happy to see me and to provide for my needs.
Her bed and her home she freely shares with me,
And she offers me love whenever I come to her.
My cup runneth over.

Surely light and love will follow me
All the days of my life
Because I have a human who loves and cares for me.

How wonderful it must be to be a beloved pet in an animal lover's home! I wished I could feel just like that, sitting here on the earth in the midst of the infinite cosmos.

Several weeks later, I was driving down the highway one day listening to one of Tim Janis's wonderful CDs, and suddenly felt a presence I can only describe as "The Magnificence"—an infinite, indescribable sense of spirit and beingness that seemed to pervade the entire universe, an intelligence directing and powering the cars around me, the people that drove them, deliveries of groceries to supermarkets, world financial markets, the growing of trees and flowers, the movement of the oceans and birds and stars and planets, overseeing everything I could imagine. I suppose this presence is what many people think of as God.

All I could think of to say was, "It's nice to meet you," as I started laughing and crying at the same time in total overwhelm. Since that time, when I play that particular song, I often feel that same presence. Sometimes I look for it and can't find it; sometimes I am desperate for it. Thinking of the idea of being a "beloved pet" to the Universe made me wonder if that presence I felt might see us in a similar way, and if, in spite of my history, I might be able to live as if I'm as well taken care of as a beloved pet.

I had always felt a version of that presence existed in cats—in the way a mother knew to lick her kittens after birth, the way cats instinctually hunted. I began to wonder: had I hid both myself and God in cats?

I began to notice that same sense of presence every now and then in my life, and came to think of it as the heart of the Universe—the same life force energy that makes plants grow, allows sentient beings to reproduce, and urges us to create again and again. Housesitting for a friend one weekend, I noticed the presence in her house, which sat on a lovely plain with a distant view of a slow-moving river. I realized that I'd rarely felt the presence in my own home—just as I'd rarely felt it at home as a child.

Over time, as I experienced this presence more and more often, I began to understand and feel its benevolence, its peace, and its unconditional, nonjudgmental regard of me—as if I might actually be a "pet" whose human antics and endeavors this presence might observe, and might possibly even appreciate and enjoy.

As I began over time to invite that presence into my private space, I found myself feeling uncertain about what it "thought" and how it "felt" about the way I conducted my life. A lot of old shame came up—feelings that I should be doing things a different way, that I wasn't good enough, that I should try harder—all of the "lessons" I had learned so well at an early age. But over time I came to perceive this presence as only an "interested party," an observer of my life and my efforts, and sometimes a helper, rather than a criticizer of how I was choosing to live my life.

The fundamentalist sect of the Protestant church that I'd been brought up in encouraged me to develop a perception in childhood that God had very strict rules by which we were supposed to abide, and that He was very difficult to please, just as my parents had been. And most of God's rules were the same ones my parents had. But in communing with this presence, I've come to believe that God is more an observer and co-creator than a judge, and this perspective has helped me to let go of a lot of old shame and guilt.

I imagine I came to this perspective as a result of thinking of life and love and the world in terms of animals instead of humans. Somehow it makes perfect sense to me to relate to everything through the perspective on my bond with cats.

It seems as if my relationship with cats is fundamental to my experience of spirituality, and I wonder if this is true for other people who love animals.

Throughout my life, I had always perceived the world—the physical universe—to be static and unchanging. In spite of their fervent religiosity, my parents were so focused on physical reality and practical issues that I assumed that was all there was. Even though I could sense all kinds of mysterious things going on under the surface of life, my parents never demonstrated a sense of anything "behind" reality, except for a very judgmental and angry God. Since everything about the church we went to was repetitive (the same songs, the same Bible verses, the same litany of the seasons), I had no reason to believe there really was anything underneath the static view of the world I developed. I thought my intuition of something powerful and loving underneath it all was just an overactive imagination.

But as I made an effort to tune into this presence, I began understanding that the Universe is as alive and mutable as cats and animals are—sometimes playing with abandon, as when the ocean tides are high and the waves fling themselves against the shoreline with unmitigated glee—sometimes restful, maybe even affectionate/happy/wild/free/creative. As I reached out with my awareness to find out if this was so, I discovered that yes, the energy around us is constantly in flux, as quantum physicists propose. There is a compelling universal symphony of flow and movement and feeling underneath the surface of our assumedly fixed "reality."

I tried to relate to this energy as if it was another being (like a cat, of course)—but that wasn't right. I tried relating to it as many beings, but that didn't feel right, either. I finally came up with a comfortable description of what's out there as "an interconnected, vibrant aliveness." I imagine this is what many people call God—in my mind, not truly a being, but an energy instead.

Finally, I could see the Universe as a reflection of Emma, which is exactly what I'd been seeking: I felt the swirling energy of atoms and molecules, the amazing symmetry of life force energy; the fierceness of lightning storms and tidal waves, the tenderness of babies and just-sprouted plants. Rather than feeling like the Universe was an unyielding physical reality that had existed just as it is even before I was born, I could now see it as a living, growing thing, constantly reaching for more and developing its potential.

Little by little, I began to feel like the Universe was taking care of me. If I had too much on my plate, something got cancelled. Things that I needed started showing up. One night, as I drove home after teaching a writing class, I felt as if the heart of the Universe was opening up to me—I sent love to it the same way I always had to Emma, and I felt its love coming back to me.

I finally realized why, though I could connect with this presence, I had never been able to relate to the idea of Jesus as a manifestation of God's love: because my primary "love" connection had always been with animals and nature and the Universe rather than human beings.

I wanted to curl up in the loving arms of the Universe the way Emma had curled up in mine. I wanted it to love me just the way I am—the same way that Emma loved me just the way I am.

I had finally reached one of my goals: knowing that the Universe can love me the way Emma loved me—and that it can be there for me always, the way Emma was.

Chapter 11: Personhood

After a time, my mourning for Emma became intertwined with mourning for my lost childhood, for the deeply loving aspect of my nature that had been so hurt when I was young.

Lying in bed one morning, comforting my inner child as tears ran down my face, I suddenly saw cats through her eyes—beautiful, loving creatures, full of life and vitality—and I realized that throughout my childhood, I had felt like a *thing* instead of a person. When I was in my mother's way, she pushed me aside as she might push aside a kitchen utensil that was in her way. When my father needed attention, he came to me as if I was just another *thing* he happened to need in that moment. When I stood in front of the TV in my footie pjs desperately wanting my mother's attention, as I wrote in my memoir *The Box of Daughter*, my mother said, "You make a better door than you do a window." When she needed help with chores, I was a tool just like the broom and the dustpan.

A poem I wrote in 1999, *The Box of Daughter*, which was the inspiration for my memoir, began with the line "When I was a little girl, I wanted more than anything to be a person. But my parents wanted me to be a daughter." Though I hadn't realized yet that I felt like I was just a *thing*, I knew I didn't feel like a person—at least not someone who had the right to live a full and complete life, expecting others to reciprocate what I gave, expecting my efforts to result in success. How can a *thing* have any impact on the world? I received my affection and respect back from cats rather than people—which may be part of why I've always felt more like a cat than a person.

I was a mirror for my parents, an emotional teddy bear that was there whenever they needed support. Lying in bed, my stomach clenched as I realized that to my parents, *I was simply a thing to be used*, like all the other things they used to make their lives better. I had lived my "real self" through my relationship with cats. But now, as I went through the process of exploring myself and the cosmos without the "interface" of cats, I could bloom into total aliveness as a person, and leave "thinghood" behind.

I could feel all of my cells singing as I lay in bed, claiming their right to life, sucking in energy and throwing out waste, each dancing to the rhythm of life, all alive, dynamic, constantly in flux, and I realized that I had felt like a lump of clay, a robot, an animated machine for most of my life. I'd been obsessed with cats because some part of me saw them as voraciously alive in comparison to my very limited self-concept.

And I began to wonder:

What if I was as much alive as I perceived cats to be?

What if I was as bright, as sweet, as full of life as Emma?

What if the Universe was as enamored of me as I was of cats?

What if my inner child could feel loved and appreciated just as much as I loved and appreciated Emma?

What would it feel like if someone in my life had been as obsessed with meeting *my* needs as I was with meeting my cats' needs?

And finally, what if a person could be as enamored of themselves as they were with anything and everything in life? Wouldn't that be high self-esteem? Giving oneself the same esteem one gives others who are searching, seeking, exploring, doing the best they can with life? Our society never encourages us to love ourselves, but I think that loving the self must be at the root of happiness, confidence, and serenity.

At last I had uncovered the root of the issue: that cats represented beings full of life and vitality in contrast to my own perception of myself—adopted from my parents—as a "thing."

No wonder I felt I couldn't live without cats.

And in the midst of the rigidity of my childhood—being forced to act in certain ways, denied expression of my inner self, having my needs ignored and my ideas and actions belittled—I had seen cats expressing themselves fully: hiding when they wanted to be left alone, playing with abandon, showing love when the spirit moved them, totally doing their own thing. So I'd always wished I could be a cat, because I thought that was the only way to fully and completely be who I was. The next best thing was always having a cat traveling with me on the road of life. Then, being a "thing" could at least be enlivened by the beauty, wisdom, and joy of cats.

I am so amazed that the human psyche can not only preserve its essence by projecting itself onto another being, but that it can also retrieve feelings and provide insights when the time for healing and the journey to wholeness arises.

I wish for myself and every person in the world the freedom to express as fully and completely as our furred and feathered friends do.

One of the things I loved most about Emma was her complete purity of being—her fearlessness and absolute nonjudgment of self in being able to say, "I want this now..." "This is how I feel now..." I'm not in the mood now..." "I'm going to sleep now..."—a complete self-acceptance of being however she was at every moment, even when she was ill. And as pets always do, Emma accepted me unconditionally as well, with all my flaws and shortcomings.

I felt that she knew me to the depths of my soul, and loved me more deeply than any human being ever had. I wondered how I could generate that kind of self-love—not an egotistical or selfish way of being, but a way of treating myself and talking to myself (psychologists call this "self-talk") that was self-accepting and loving.

For most of my life, I've been what Dr. Clarissa Pinkola Estes calls an "Unmothered Child." And I suspect that I came from a long line of unmothered children, which was why my parents were so needy. So I had to learn how to mother myself.

One night, I was listening to Peter Kater's "Compassion," and suddenly the pain of Emma's loss hit me full on. As the tears ran down my face, I talked to my inner child, as I often did when she was sad, telling her I was sorry, and that I loved her, and wished I could take the pain away. Since my parents had rarely acknowledged or soothed my pain, years before Emma's death I'd learned to do that for myself. It made life as a "thing" more bearable.

Suddenly I realized that in that moment I was relating to my inner child as I'd related to Emma—as a sweet, vulnerable, loving, affectionate, natural being. For a few moments, I felt in communion with both Emma's spirit and my inner child, and they seemed to merge into one and the same. I knew in that moment that I had reclaimed my deepest self, the part of me that had to "hide inside cats" because life hurt too much.

One cold winter day as I sat cozily at home working on a jigsaw puzzle, my inner child noticed a parrot off to the side of the jungle scene. I felt immediate interest: "I'd like to have a parrot as a pet!" Another part of my mind piped up, "What about cats? Aren't we going to get a cat once we settle in a new place?" Oddly, the thought of getting another cat—as much as I missed Emma and love cats—made my inner child a little jealous that I might be giving all the love and care I'd been giving to her to a new cat—and she would be left once again with no one to love her.

In that moment, my suspicion that I had always loved cats so much because my inner child felt vicariously loved when I gave love to cats was confirmed. But apparently that young aspect of my psyche was much happier experiencing my love for her firsthand. I truly wanted to treat myself as gently and care for myself as much as I did for Emma.

But why couldn't I have both? As much as I enjoyed this newfound connection with myself and the Universe, I began to wonder if perhaps this connection could actually be enhanced by the presence of a cat.

I redoubled my efforts to find a new place to live that would allow me to have a beloved cat once again.

Chapter 12: Reunion

Time has a way of passing without our even noticing. More than two years went by before I could consider getting another cat. I had finally moved to a new space that allowed pets, and as soon as I felt reasonably settled in the new house, I started looking around for a cat companion.

I began visiting shelters, amazed at the variety of cats who had ended up without homes. Though I wasn't looking for a cat exactly like Emma, I did want to find one who reminded me of her beauty and dignity in some way.

Cats are like people in that they have different personalities: some seem to approach life with humor, acting out with amusing behaviors; some seem peaceful and quiet, like furry little Buddhas; and some express the drama of cathood—making flying leaps to catch toys, acting as if each moment is full of the vitality and elation of life itself.

I developed a relationship with the local animal shelter, going every week or two to visit and check out the felines looking for homes. I was a little gun-shy. After more than two years without a cat, I was very mindful that once I got one, it was a very long-term commitment. And I knew I had a tendency to be drawn to the runt of the litter—my heart cried every time I saw a skinny, abandoned-looking animal, or one with some illness that had to be taken care of and restored to health. So I wanted to be mindful in my search.

I was hoping to find a gray tabby with tortoiseshell markings like Emma, even though I knew personalities could be quite different, but so far I hadn't seen one. One day on a whim, I went to a different shelter, one that I hadn't been to in months because it was a half hour away. As I walked into the cat room, a lovely lady with markings very similar to Emma's stood up in her cage, arched her neck the same way Emma used to, and rubbed her face on the bars as if she was greeting me after waiting for me for a long time. Memories of Emma flooded my mind.

I stood and watched her for a few minutes, then I went to the desk to ask if I could take her out and visit. She came willingly into my arms, and then asked to get down and explore. Her coat looked healthy; she was a year and a half old, and had only been in the shelter for two days. I enjoyed watching her canvass the room for a while before I put her back in the cage, and then I watched her for awhile longer before moving on to look at the other cats.

I'm not sure what it is, but often I get a sense of the "soul" of a particular cat—kind of a combination of personality, intelligence, self-awareness, and other-awareness. Kya had a presence that the other cats there definitely lacked. Someday I hope I can put my finger on what I'm sensing.

I asked at the desk if they knew why she'd been brought in. "Two brothers brought her in—they just said there was poop all over the place," the attendant told me. I figured that meant a home where many cats lived and the litter boxes were infrequently cleaned. At least it didn't sound like there had been trauma in her background, the way there had been with Emma. And Kya hadn't responded with fear when I took her into my arms.

Watching Kya, I was in full freak-out mode, my thoughts bouncing wildly back and forth between "I can really finally get a cat!" and "What a huge commitment this will be. Am I sure I'm ready for it?" She looked so much like Emma that deja vu swept over me.

Being older and wiser offers many positive blessings, but sometimes it makes decisions so much more difficult!

Though part of me wanted to grab Kya and run, I told myself I would sleep on it and come back the next day if I wanted her, even though the shelter was quite a distance from where I lived. On the drive back, my mind ran at a hysterical pace, trying to make this decision that seemed so huge.

I got halfway home, and my inner child wanted to cry. "Soul mate," she said. I kept hearing the words "soul mate" in my head. My inner world turned into a bleak landscape of dashed hopes as emptiness flooded my heart. The force of my needs swamped my frantic cogitation about what I should or shouldn't do, and in a split second, I turned around to go back and get Kya.

When I got back to the shelter and told them I wanted to adopt her, we went to get her, and another woman was standing a little ways away from the cage. When she saw the attendant taking Kya from her cage, she said, "I was just thinking about adopting her." I still marvel at whatever it was that made me turn around and go back just in time to adopt her before someone else did. And what had made me decide to visit that shelter that day, with only a two-day window in which to meet her? Synchronicity always makes me shiver, and I love that the Universe provides us with experiences of brilliant timing.

Part of me was ecstatic to have a cat in my life again, but part of me was shouting, "What am I doing? Now I have to clean the litter box and put food down and take her to the vet..." One of the major challenges of my life is that I often have conflicting desires, probably because of the trauma of my childhood and the fact that I'm still integrating aspects of myself that have been hidden for most of my life. I've grown up in fits and starts, wanting so many things in my life that it's hard for me to go in just one direction.

When I brought Kya home, she explored the house with as much zeal as she had shown at the shelter. Then she settled down contentedly to eat. The first few days, as we got to know each other, I noticed that she would flinch and blink if I moved toward her too fast, or put my hand too close to her face, and I wondered if there was any abuse in her past. It seemed unlikely that she would have been abused in a home with many cats—in my experience, those homes are usually owned by a human who dearly loves cats.

But after cleaning the litter box a few times, and remembering the attendant's comment, I wondered if someone had given her up because of diarrhea—loose stools most of the time, and one explosive experience that required a little wall-cleaning. I knew from personal experience that stress could cause digestive problems, and I knew that being in the shelter had probably been extremely stressful for Kya, so I still wanted to give her a chance. It's so easy sometimes to forgive our animal companions, as they forgive us. I was really enjoying getting to know her, and I wasn't about to give her up without a longer trial.

I started experimenting with food to help her digestive system, and it turned out that several varieties of fish-based cat food were the culprits. When I completely removed fish from her diet, including the dry food I fed her that contained fish, the problem was totally resolved.

It also turned out that she had never been fixed. In the midst of a play session one day, I got a whiff of what I can only describe as "cat musk." When I called the shelter to confirm what my nose was telling me, the attendant said, "Oh, right, it's not in the record. Usually we spay cats before they're adopted, but she wasn't here that long." They gave me the name of their vet, and said they would pay for the procedure, which was very kind of them. I took her in the next week.

I learned to move toward Kya slowly, and she accepted a bit of petting at first, but would quickly turn and bite me—not too hard—after just a minute or two. I said, "No biting!", but I also respected her need to say "That's enough!" I know that petting can be overstimulating for sensitive cats, in the same way that life is sometimes overstimulating to people like me who are hyperaware.

Over the next few weeks, as we continued our mutual training, the length of time I could pet her stretched longer and longer, and her urge to bite seemed to dissipate. Now that I've had her for nearly a year, she happily plops on her side, just the way Emma did, to enjoy chin-scratching, head-rubbing, and general petting. And her "bites" have morphed into simply turning her head and opening her mouth to let me know she's had enough.

As Kya has become more affectionate, I'm constantly amazed at how much she's like Emma. When she's relaxed and I scratch her neck, her paws open and close as if she's kneading. She enjoys ear massage—when I grasp her ears at the base, and pull slightly. She's infinitely patient in waiting for me to put food down, and rarely meows. She gives me lots of head-butts, and even licks my fingers sometimes. She's not especially comfortable sitting in my lap, but enjoys lying on my chest and stomach when I'm lying down, a position that Skippy usually preferred. Kya doesn't like to be picked up and doesn't like her tummy touched. So many similarities... I've often wondered if our animal friends reincarnate in order to renew and strengthen the loving bond they have with their humans, and one particular experience with Kya made me into a believer.

A few weeks after Kya came to live with me, I was putting some clean clothes away in the dresser. Kya saw the drawer open, and her whole body came to attention as she nosed her way into the drawer, immediately going for the back of it to see if there was a hidey-hole to crawl into. I stood, awestruck, watching as she pushed at the back of the drawer with her paw, peered into the darkness behind the drawer, and tried to wiggle her paw into the narrow slot at the back of it. When that didn't work, she went under the dresser, as Emma had when she crawled into her special space.

My breath caught. Watching Kya at that moment pretty much convinced me that she's the same kitty soul which inhabited the bodies of Skippy and Emma.

Apparently, the name "Kya" in the African language means "A diamond in the sky." I can't help but think of Emma's soul residing like a star in the heavens until she decided to return in kitty form.

As my relationship with Kya has developed, I've felt my inner child's happiness grow, as if she finally feels like she's found her soul mate. And the funny thing is, I've started to feel whole again. Living with a cat is like having my "other half" back in my life.

And I wonder: How could I have lived for more than two years without this incredible experience? Unwinding after work by playing cat and mouse and string and bird; waking on a slow morning, running my hands over a purring ball of fur next to me; basking in a smile of bliss when I scratch Kya's white chin; laughing at her leaps and jumps and pounces; taking in her rubs and head-butts.

Apparently, I need a cat to help me feel that the Universe is in perfect order. Kya's steadiness and steadfastness helps me to heal from the chaos of life with my parents.

I've come to the realization that despite my experiment to develop a deeper relationship with other people and the Universe and learn to love myself more, I still need cats because the child-aspect of my psyche needs unconditional love from a totally nonjudgmental "other" in order to feel that life is worth living. That aspect of myself never learned to receive unconditional love from people, much as I try to bring her along in my journey of life. And that depth of unconditional love between adults seems rare.

As I continue to grow and heal from the past, I hope to be able to bring that aspect of myself more fully into my relationship with others and the Universe. But for now, that part of me is happy in a way that nothing else I've found will give her.

When I come home, Kya hears my car and jumps up in the kitchen window to greet me on my way to the front door, scratching at the glass and rubbing her face on the window shade. Sometimes she leaves her favorite toy bird just in front of the door, as if she's left me a present from her indoor hunt. There's nothing like being greeted with complete affection, as if a pet has had the most wonderful day, and you're the person they most want to see.

That's what I always wanted from my mother. But at least I've found it with my pets.

It seems that, though many aspects of childhood loss can be healed, perhaps the core of the self, developed in the years even before words, remains dependent on whatever mother-substitutes we might have found.

My relationships with animals and nature have always encouraged me to expand and grow, to become the best that I can be. Animals teach us how to love in ways that we may not even be able to teach each other. They can help us change our life perspective if we choose to, and in the process, develop new relationships with ourselves, with others, and with All That Is. I'm so grateful to Emma and Kya for showing me how infinite the experience of loving and being loved can be.

And when Kya sits on my lap, her blissful expression shining love into my heart, I see her wild, tender beauty as a part of me, and I feel like I have finally come home.

About the Author

A former actress who appeared Off-Broadway and on the daytime drama Guiding Light, Katherine Mayfield is the author of the award-winning memoir *The Box of Daughter: Healing the Authentic Self* and *What's Your Story? – A Quick Guide to Writing Your Memoir*. She's also published a guide to recovery from bullying for teens and adults, called *Bullied: Why You Feel Bad Inside and What to Do About It*; a book for people who experience family bullying, *Stand Your Ground*; a book of essays, *The Meandering Muse*; a book of poetry, *The Box of Daughter & Other Poems*; and other books on recovery from dysfunctional family dynamics. She has spoken at schools, libraries, and conventions on the subjects of recovery from bullying and creating an authentic life.

Ms. Mayfield's memoir *The Box of Daughter* won awards in the Reader's Favorite Book Awards and the New England Book Festival. Ms. Mayfield has presented writing workshops and taught memoir classes in Maine, New Hampshire, and Massachusetts, and teaches memoir-writing online at www.Katherine-Mayfield.com/eclass.htm.

Websites and Social Media:
www.TheBoxofDaughter.com
www.Katherine-Mayfield.com
Twitter: K_Mayfield   Facebook: KatherineMayfieldauthor

CPSIA information can be obtained
at www.ICGtesting.com
Printed in the USA
BVHW091800070119
537207BV00020B/1606/P

9 780997 612165